Redeeming America

REDEEMING AMERICA

Evangelicals and the Road to Civil War

Curtis D. Johnson

The American Ways Series

IVAN R. DEE   *Chicago*

Library of Congress Cataloging-in-Publication Data:
Johnson, Curtis D., 1949–
    Redeeming America : evangelicals are the road to civil war /
Curtis D. Johnson.
       p.   cm. — (The American ways series)
    Includes bibliographical references and index.
    ISBN 1-56663-031-2 (cloth : alk. paper). — ISBN 1-56663-032-0
(paper : alk. paper)
    1. Evangelicalism—United States—History—19th century.
2. United States—History—Civil War, 1861–1865—Religions aspects. 3. United States—Church history—19th century. I. Title.
II. Series.
BR1644.5.U6J64   1993
277.3'081—dc20   93-11242

Contents

Preface

THIS BOOK explores the impact of evangelical Protestantism on antebellum American culture. In so doing it synthesizes much of the scholarship on this topic that has been produced over several decades.

Evangelicalism before the Civil War must be first understood as a religious system before it can be analyzed as a social phenomenon. Historians have long recognized that defining evangelicals theologically is a formidable task. I also realize the pitfalls in trying to characterize a movement well known for its amorphous social and religious boundaries. Yet the failure to look at what distinguished evangelical thought can lead to an equally serious problem—the tendency to explain a religious movement by examining its social components, without giving adequate attention to the ideas that energized and shaped the movement in the first place.

Redeeming America is structured around five theological ideas that evangelicals upheld with great seriousness. At the same time this book recognizes that social location played an important role in shaping how evangelicals interpreted the five doctrines. Thus each chapter discusses how formal evangelicals (usually middle- to upper-class whites), anti-formal evangelicals (usually lower- to middle-class whites), and African American evangelicals interpreted the five central principles. The debates over the meaning and application of these evangelical doctrines ultimately had an enormous impact on American culture.

Books are written in communities, not in isolation. Like

other authors, I owe a large debt to friends and colleagues whose assistance I acknowledge here. I thank Mount Saint Mary's College for a year-long sabbatical to write the manuscript and Thomas Flynn for his enthusiastic support of the project from its inception to its completion. Lisa Sachs pariently typed numerous drafts, and Lisa Davis obtained dozens of key documents through interlibrary loan. Conversations with André Smith led to many insights and a greater understanding of the African American experience. Members of the Mason-Dixon history seminar critiqued chapter two and made many helpful comments. Robert Olwell and Richard Shiels generously read the manuscript and made important stylistic, bibliographic, and interpretative suggestions which I have since incorporated. I also thank John Braemen and Ivan Dee, first for the opportunity to write a volume in American Ways series and second, for their heroic efforts in helping me produce a succinct, polished text. Finally I thank my wife, Lita, for her thoughtful comments, editorial advice, and unfailing support while this manuscript became a reality.

C. D. J.

Emmitsburg, Maryland
May 1993

Redeeming America

Introduction

IN 1831 ALEXIS DE TOCQUEVILLE, a young French aristo-
crat, landed in the United States with the intention of
discovering what made American society work. "On my
arrival in the United States," Tocqueville noted, "the religious aspect of the country was the first thing that struck my
attention." What Tocqueville found most interesting was
American religion's unofficial yet highly important role.
"Religion in America takes no direct part in the government
of society, but it must be regarded as the first of their
political institutions. . . . I do not know whether all Americans have a sincere faith in their religion . . . but I am certain
that they hold it to be indispensable to the maintenance of
republican institutions. This opinion is not peculiar to a class
of citizens or to a party, but it belongs to the whole nation
and to every rank of society."

Although he did not realize it, Tocqueville entered the
United States at the peak of a huge religious revival later
called the Second Great Awakening. Evangelical Protestants
were the driving force behind American religious renewal.
By the time of the Civil War, scarcely an American institution was untouched by their enthusiasm. Education, politics,
gender roles, leisure activities, and the slavery debate—all
were influenced by the evangelical imagination. Americans,
whether thinking of themselves as individuals or as a people,
developed their self-understanding largely in terms of evangelical thought. Overall, between the years 1820 and 1860

evangelical Protestants had a greater impact on American culture than at any time before or since.

The importance of evangelicalism is surprising when one realizes that in this era only about a fourth of the adult population were evangelical church members and only about a third of all Americans regularly worshiped in an evangelical church. On the eve of the Civil War there were roughly four million evangelical church members out of a population that approximated thirty million. But membership totals alone understate the evangelical impact. If children, seekers, and casual attenders are added to the official membership, the number of Americans under direct evangelical influence swelled to about 60 percent of the population. By contrast, Catholics influenced about 15 percent, nonevangelical Protestants* affected another 10 percent, and Jews comprised less than 1 percent of the population. The remaining 15 percent of Americans had no religious affiliation at all.

But the influence of evangelicalism was not simply a matter of numbers. Nineteenth-century evangelicals drew their strength from a religion that was qualitatively different from much religion today. In the twentieth century the sacred and secular are often far apart. Many church members in our era infrequently attend, cannot distinguish their religious group from others, are unaware of their church's teachings on most subjects, and thus are essentially unaffected by the religion to which they belong. By contrast, antebellum evangelicals of all camps agreed that one's faith should shape one's behavior, not just on Sunday but during the entire week, in all phases of life.

*Nonevangelical Protestants included primarily Unitarians, Universalists, High Church Episcopalians, Quakers, Mormons, most Lutherans, and members of certain German sects.

Evangelical beliefs were at the core of evangelical behavior on issues ranging from education to gender and race. People consciously chose to be evangelical; one could not simply be born into the faith or receive full membership upon confirmation. (Granted, some choices were not carefully thought out and merely mimicked the decisions of parents or friends. But the demands of living the evangelical life-style meant that casual believers would either recommit themselves or later drop out of the church.) Evangelicals believed their faith was the most important tool they owned in separating truth from error, in determining right and wrong, and for providing meaning and purpose during their earthly sojourn. As a result, if we want to understand their behavior we must look at what nineteenth-century evangelicals believed.

In common with the vast majority of Christians of that day, evangelicals believed in the divinity of Jesus, Christ's atonement for the sins of humanity, the Resurrection of Jesus, and the Last Judgment. But evangelicals were at the same time a distinct group within American Christianity. The broadest *definition* of evangelicalism includes everyone who believed that the Second Birth was essential for salvation—that no one could enter heaven without a conscious emotional experience in which he accepted God's grace and dedicated his entire being to his glory. Unlike sacramentalists,* evangelicals believed that baptism and the Lord's Supper were not means of divine grace but were symbolic rituals to be performed in obedience to biblical commands.

*Sacramentalists are groups such as Catholics, High Church Episcopalians, Lutherans, and the Eastern Orthodox who believe that God's grace comes primarily through sacraments such as baptism and the Eucharist, not through individual conversion experiences.

This lowest-common-denominator definition does not include other factors that made antebellum evangelicals historically important. Four additional ideas profoundly shaped evangelical behavior. In some cases the ideas themselves differed from those of other Christians; in other instances evangelicals emphasized the ideas far more than other Christian groups. In addition to the Second Birth, evangelicals subscribed to *Sola Scriptura,* or the idea that the Bible alone had authority over Christian faith and life. While Lutherans agreed with this point, other sacramentalists believed that reason, tradition, and church authority played equally important roles in defining the Christian faith. Second, evangelicals maintained that Christians must live a just and holy life, partly as a sign of obedience to God and partly to demonstrate that their conversion experience was genuine. Generally they defined the Christian life in far more precise (and rigid) terms than their more relaxed nineteenth-century counterparts. Third, they sought to redeem America, to make the United States a truly Christian nation. While some sacramentalists (such as Catholics Orestes Brownson and Isaac Hecker) acted on this desire, most were content to live out their faith within their own ethnic group or religious community. Finally, evangelicals believed in the Second Coming of Christ and spent enormous effort speculating on how the Second Advent would occur. By contrast, sacramentalists accepted this doctrine but were not overly concerned with the details surrounding this event.

As much as American evangelicals were shaped by doctrine, they were also influenced by the same social factors that affect all of us. Just like other people, they were affected by their social location. The central argument of this book is that while they shared five distinctive ideas (*Sola Scriptura,* the Second Birth, the need for a just and holy life, a desire to redeem America, and the Second Coming), evangelicals occupied three different positions in society and, as a result, they interpreted the five central doctrines differently. Consequently, nineteenth-century evangelicals were highly diverse despite their essential agreement on matters of doctrine. The debate among evangelicals over the five ideas set off major conflicts that spilled over into political and cultural arenas, and these differences influenced the shape of American society in the period between 1820 and 1860.

Antebellum evangelicals can be organized into three major groups.

Formalists, who comprised about one-fifth of evangelical church members, were most often Congregationalists, Presbyterians, Low Church Episcopalians, and English-speaking Reformed groups. Drawing their strength from the middle and upper classes, these white evangelicals sought an *orderly* faith which stressed consistent doctrine, decorum in worship, and biblical interpretation through a well-educated ministry. Formal evangelicals were most powerful in the commercial and cultural center of the nation, the Northeast. Frequently at the center of local and national politics, formalists often sought to extend religious and social order to the rest of the nation through a network of voluntary associations known as the "benevolent empire." Their ultimate goal was to create a self-disciplined Righteous Republic whose laws reflected the edicts of God.

Antiformalists, who made up three-fifths of evangelical church members, were generally Methodists, Baptists, and "Christians" or Disciples of Christ. Antiformal evangelicals came primarily from the lower and middle classes. Compared with formalists, these white evangelicals were strongest in the South and West and were socially and economically weaker. They sought an *emotional* faith that could not be controlled or manipulated by their well-educated "social betters." In addition, antiformalists were deeply suspicious of elite attempts to Christianize society, to reform the nation, or in any other way to improve America. To their way of thinking, a Christian Republic would be realized only when individuals were converted, one by one, to a right relationship with God.

African Americans, with about one-fifth of evangelical church membership, most frequently were Methodists and Baptists. Socially and politically they were at the bottom of society; most were enslaved, and the remainder encountered severe prejudice. Yet as a community African Americans sought a *liberating* faith which would maximize their spiritual and material well-being. By including African customs within Christianity, black evangelicals forged an evangelical belief system that sustained them during slavery, encouraged resistance to slaveholding ideology, helped them carve out a sphere of spiritual autonomy, and pointed forward to the Jubilee when God would emancipate his people. Only when slavery and racial injustice were destroyed could America become a Christian nation.

To a degree this threefold classification is idealized. Non-evangelicals could be found in evangelical denominations, and evangelicals could be found in nonevangelical groups. The degree of formality within each of the three groups varied greatly, usually in response to region and urbanization. Within each group the most formal members lived in the North or in cities. The least formal were in the South and in rural areas. As a result, many Northern Baptists preferred highly educated ministers and refined worship despite their antiformal origins. Similarly, Southern Presbyterians gravitated toward the enthusiastic pulpit-pounding of antiformal Methodists and Baptists. Among black evangelicals, African religious practices were predominant in the rural South and were less common among black congregations in the urban North. Groups also had a tendency to formalize with time. As Northern antiformalists became more wealthy, more educated, and more urban between 1820 and 1860, they increased their emphasis on organized activity and became embarrassed by open displays of raw religious passion, preferring domesticated emotions instead. African American religion drifted more slowly toward formalism, as Southern slavery and Northern discrimination kept most blacks from experiencing wealth, education, or urban life.

The more difficult question is why evangelical groups were the dominant religious force in America between 1820 and 1860. Two reasons are particularly important. First, the disestablishment of religion in the late eighteenth and early nineteenth centuries—that is, the end of state support for specific groups—leveled the playing field among Christian denominations. Second, the diversity of evangelicalism made it possible to meet the different and conflicting needs of the heterogeneous American population.

Disestablishment had profound consequences for religion in the new republic. If the United States was to be in any sense a Christian nation, the source of its religiosity would have to be the people, not the state. Joining a church was voluntary, not a requirement. Which church one joined, if any, was clearly in the realm of democratic choice. By 1831 the voluntaristic nature of American religion was so well established that Alexis de Tocqueville wrote that the United States "was peopled by men who, after having shaken off the

authority of the Pope, acknowledged no other religious
supremacy: they brought with them into the New World a
form of Christianity which I cannot better describe than by
styling it a democratic and republican religion."

When the state no longer supported a specific church, the
most successful denominations were those that most vigorously recruited members. About 90 percent of the American
people had no formal religious affiliation in 1800, which
meant that any denomination seeking to attract a significant
portion of the unaffiliated had to be aggressive in propagating its views, with an effective organizational strategy for
spreading its ideas and a message that offered meaning and
a sense of belonging.

Some denominations were at a competitive disadvantage.
Anglicans had to overcome the stigma of their British
heritage, a severe handicap in postrevolutionary America.
Even after Anglicans in the United States renamed themselves Episcopalians in 1789, they were seen as too elitist and
too formal in liturgy by most Americans, who favored a
more popular and spontaneous religiosity. Catholics were
few, and, recognizing the Protestant majority's strong opposition to "papist" religion, chose to keep a low profile rather
than to evangelize. Lutherans failed to break past barriers of
language and ethnicity to make a large impact on other
Americans.

In contrast to the above groups, evangelical denominations
were ideally posed to fill the religious vacuum in the new
nation. Each claimed to be genuinely American, evangelized
aggressively, and presented a message with broad appeal.

Each evangelical group trumpeted its Americanness. Congregationalists were the descendants of Pilgrims and Puritans, the dominant religious force in New England from the
early 1600s. Baptists traced their roots to Roger Williams,

founder of Rhode Island and advocate of church-state separation. Presbyterians had a long history in the Middle Colonies where Gilbert Tennent played a crucial role in the Great Awakening of the 1740s. The Methodists, who until 1784 were a subgroup within the Anglican church, were occasionally attacked because of their British ties. But their theology, informal style of worship, and vigorous evangelism was so unlike the Anglicans that accusations of being pro-British lost their potency by the early 1800s. Some of the newer sects, such as the Disciples of Christ, were founded in America and adapted their message to the American cultural environment even more successfully than the older denominations.

The evangelical denominations aggressively evangelized a nation that was rapidly moving west. Between 1790 and 1840 more than four million people moved beyond the Appalachians. This figure is larger than the entire American population during the American Revolution. The denominations that followed Americans westward were the ones that prospered over time. In 1801 Presbyterians and Congregationalists formed a Plan of Union which merged their missionary efforts so they would never compete against each other in the same community. This agreement eliminated duplication of effort and made it possible for both groups to maximize their resources. Baptists spread their faith through state missionary societies in Massachusetts and New York, a national General Missionary Convention, and farmer-preachers sponsored by individual congregations. The Methodist Episcopal church could be viewed as one huge missionary society that sent itinerant ministers, known as circuit riders, from community to community throughout the West.

Evangelicals recruited successfully because they had a message with broad appeal. Although they shared the same doctrines, formal, antiformal, and African American evangelicals interpreted them differently, thus addressing the different needs and circumstances of the American population.

After 1820 formal evangelicals had their greatest success among people who were comfortable with the modern commercial economy that was developing within the United States, most strikingly in the Northern states. In the aftermath of the War of 1812, industrialization grew rapidly. Better transportation simultaneously transformed agriculture from subsistence farming to growing staple crops for sale in distant markets.

Commercialization did more than encourage Northern industry and agricultural specialization: it also rewarded new habits of mind. Men became increasingly market-driven as they engaged in economic competition against people hundreds of miles away. To succeed in trade, men had to discard the patterns of the past and become future-oriented. What was acceptable one day was not necessarily good enough the next; therefore ambitious men had to aggressively pursue education, innovation, and new political and economic alliances. Because one's parents and one's community did not necessarily understand the new order, young entrepreneurs needed to be self-reliant and inner-directed, choosing for themselves which strategies would ultimately bring financial rewards. No strategy could succeed, however, unless young men had self-control and discipline in regard to drinking, prostitutes, gambling, and other temptations.

Women were similarly affected by the marketplace. As their direct economic role declined, their moral importance grew. Commercialization tended to remove women from economic production as farmers increasingly purchased products their wives used to make at home, and as urban manufacturers and professionals engaged in work that was physically distant from the home. But as their focus shifted from production to nurture, middle-class women believed they had an increased moral responsibility to teach their children the inner-direction and self-discipline necessary for future success.

Evangelical religion expanded in the North partly because it promoted values that paralleled those of this new commercialized world. Most evangelicals taught that individuals were saved through their own personal choice, not by baptism (their parents' choice) and not by election (God's choice). Evangelicals also believed that the Holy Spirit and the church community could give believers the strength to avoid unholy (and unproductive) activities. Women became evangelicals partly because the church was a place where they could exercise authority outside the home and because the church promoted values in men that enhanced the physical and economic safety of women. Evangelical women demonstrated their own future orientation when they encouraged their children to seek salvation, a decision which would make their offspring more productive on earth and blessed in the hereafter.

When Northerners who were attracted by evangelical religion joined a church, those who were at the power center of their community and the most comfortable with the emerging commercial order gravitated toward the formalist camp. Formalists revered education and provided well-trained professional clergy. Worship was dignified, restrained, and controlled. By nineteenth-century standards, local formalist congregations were complex institutions with a host of organizations ranging from missionary societies to Sunday Schools and choirs, each emphasizing its own version of self-discipline and self-improvement. Many members also chose to improve society through voluntary religious and moral activism. When appropriate, formalists also sought the support of the government to aid their moral (but not narrowly religious) causes. Education, dignity, personal and social improvement, voluntarism, and state involvement in worthy causes were valued by those who were at the center of the new commercial order, for they promoted habits of mind essential to success.

Unlike the formal evangelicals, antiformalist evangelicalism appealed most strongly to Americans located on the margins of society. Instead of emphasizing values and habits linked to commercialization, antiformalists harkened back to an older democratic tradition of the American republic. After the Revolution many Americans took pride in their country's commitment to equality and self-government. Such sentiments were particularly strong among workingmen in the cities and struggling farmers in the interior regions. These republicans were militantly egalitarian by the standards of their day. Having recently won a war for liberty, frontier and poorer urban men and women were unwilling to allow any authority to encroach on their freedom. Even drinking took on a democratic aura as whiskey was referred to as "the spirits of independence." Should a traveler refuse to imbibe with his compatriots at a local tavern, he was often viewed as "aristocratic" and "too good for his fellows" —whiskey was forcibly poured down his throat. The drive to democratize peaked in the 1820s as most states rejected the property requirement for voting. In the view of the majority, every adult white male was as good as any other adult white male, and therefore all were equally qualified for the franchise.

Methodists, Baptists, and the Disciples of Christ were highly successful in the nineteenth century because their message mirrored the democratic impulse in the larger society. All three groups argued that individual believers could interpret the Bible for themselves without the aid of an elite, well-educated clergy. Even those who could not read could get God's message directly because, as Methodists in particular taught, God spoke to his people directly through visions and dreams. Preachers in these traditions glorified their own lack of education, spoke in the vernacular with homespun wisdom, and equated well-educated Congregational and Presbyterian clergy with Eastern elites seeking to control the weak and downtrodden. The Methodists went furthest in placing people's spiritual fates in their own hands. Methodists argued that each person could choose to be saved. This doctrine, called Arminianism, differed from the Calvinist doctrine of predestination which stated that God alone chose the eternal fate of all human beings. In each case these religious populists castigated the perpetrators of elite religion and sought to put religious authority in the hands of ordinary folk.

Antiformal evangelicals were particularly critical of the formal evangelicals and the emerging commercial class. Those on the social margins were suspicious of powerful elites who used government to promote economic policies that disproportionately benefited the commercial class. The United States Bank, the protective tariff, and taxes for internal improvements were all seen as conspiracies designed to pull money from rural, Southern, and poorer folk into the hands of urban, Northern elites. Likewise, antiformalists believed that formalist efforts to discourage alcohol consumption, to regulate the Sabbath, to ban dueling, and to eliminate other common vices were attacks on the freedom of ordinary folk to live as they pleased.

Like white evangelicalism, the African American version

of the faith grew after 1820. Stolen from their ancestral homes, African Americans sought a religion that would empower them in the New World. The logical choice would be those religions Africans brought with them to America. But by 1760 the institution of slavery had destroyed the ability of African religions to function as comprehensive systems in the New World. The theology was gone, yet African practices remained.

Many African Americans filled their theological void by combining antiformal evangelical ideas with African religious practices. African Americans were receptive to Methodist and Baptist preaching partly because both denominations criticized slavery in the late 1700s and early 1800s. In addition, blacks also were open to antiformalism because it allowed the continuation of African cultural practices. Methodists and Baptists were democratically oriented and allowed local congregations wide latitude in worship and encouraged lay leadership. Black evangelicals seized this opportunity and included in their Sunday services call-and-response community involvement, the ring shout, and African music in the form of spirituals, all led by a preacher-storyteller. Like Africans, Methodists believed that God spoke to people in dreams. Baptists believed that after conversion, each believer should be baptized through immersion. Africans whose pre-diaspora beliefs included the idea that rivers had unique holy, healing, and cleansing powers found total immersion appealing.

Unlike the religion which the planters wanted slaves to adopt, African American evangelicalism did not meekly accept the temporal status quo. At the very least, slaves and free blacks held slaveowners up to biblical standards of morality and frequently let masters know when they failed to meet God's standards. In addition, evangelicalism supported the slaves' radical critique of the unjust status quo: as one maid told her mistress, "God never made us to be slaves for white people." African American evangelicalism always created psychological space for blacks, frequently was a means of resistance, and on occasion provided support for outright rebellion.

Antebellum evangelicalism was clearly a varied movement. The chapters that follow will show how five central evangelical doctrines were interpreted differently by formal, antiformal, and African American evangelicals. The consequences of their social position on interpretation were crucial, not only for evangelicalism but for American culture as well.

1

People of the Word

AT THE CENTER of the evangelical belief structure was the concept—derived from Martin Luther—of *Sola Scriptura*, the idea that the Bible alone had authority regarding the Christian faith and that individual believers did not have to go through a priest but could communicate directly with God. That conviction would come to have a major impact on American culture and even on politics.

Although emphasizing the importance of access by everyone to the Word of God, sixteenth-century Protestant leaders never intended that believers should be free to interpret the Bible however they pleased. Accordingly, popular translations of the Bible always had extensive comments, usually written in the margins next to the corresponding texts, so that Christians would be guided in their interpretation of Scripture as they read.

Initially Puritans continued the Reformed tradition of including extensive commentary in the margins of each Bible. The adoption by Puritan leaders of the King James Authorized Version as their Bible of choice by the time the Massachusetts Bay Colony was founded in 1630 represented a major shift of policy. The King James Version, which lacked any interpretive commentary, opened the door to a host of interpretations. Nevertheless, Puritan leaders still

believed they could structure their society to prevent hetero-
doxy. First, they established Puritanism as the only legitimate
religion in New England. Initially non-Puritan preaching
was subject to banishment or death. Second, the collective
clergy claimed to have the sole power of biblical interpretation. In effect, New England's ministers sought to
provide a "living commentary" which gave an interpretive
structure to the biblical narrative. Third, because interpreting Scripture correctly had enormous consequences for this
life and the hereafter, Massachusetts established Harvard
College in 1636 to ensure an ongoing, properly educated
clergy. Fourth, New England's orthodoxy was further protected in the 1640s when English Puritans wrote the Westminster Confession which succinctly summarized the teachings
of the Puritan church. The Confession was quickly adopted
in the New England colonies.

As time went on, the Puritans struggled against powerful
forces that undercut their religious monopoly. After 1660
immigrants entering New England were increasingly diverse. The Great Awakening, a series of religious revivals
which swept the colonies between 1720 and 1770, weakened
clerical authority as itinerant preachers argued that a converted heart, not merely an educated head, was necessary to
preach the gospel. Soon after the awakening subsided, the
colonies were racked by political disturbances which culmi-
nated in the American Revolution.

In the postrevolutionary era the door was open to new
ways of approaching the Bible. Most Americans viewed the
Anglican church as an unholy remnant of British tyranny.
And state-supported Congregationalism was increasingly on
the defensive even in New England. After the war Americans were much less likely to defer to their social "betters,"

and clerical claims to authority on the basis of superior education often fell on deaf ears.

By 1820 American evangelicals professed allegiance to *Sola Scriptura*, which placed the Bible as the only authority over Christian doctrine and daily practice. In accordance with the importance of Scripture, evangelicals made the sermon the focal point of each worship service. This emphasis on preaching made Sunday worship different from that of many nonevangelical Christians who saw the homily only as the prelude to the high point of the service, the administering of the Eucharist.

Beyond the shared emphasis on Holy Writ, antebellum evangelicals disagreed sharply on how to interpret the Word of God. Formal evangelicals, building on a tradition that began with the Puritans, argued that the Bible could best be understood by those who possessed a classical education. This meant that Congregational, Presbyterian, and evangelical-minded Episcopal clergy were the nation's most qualified expositors and that American evangelicals should follow their teaching. Within this framework, which placed supreme emphasis on intellect and education, the Holy Spirit principally acted upon the minister in his study. By contrast, Baptists, Methodists, and the Disciples of Christ sought to overthrow the tyranny of creeds, clergy, and elite education over the interpretation of Scripture. Antiformalists believed the Bible was a plain book and that with the help of the Holy Spirit and common sense, each person could read and interpret it correctly. In addition, the Holy Spirit occasionally supplemented Scripture by giving believers dreams and visions. Black evangelicals drew heavily on such African traditions as storytelling, memorization, and community interpretation in their use of Scripture. In addition, the Holy

Spirit played an important role in guiding the daily lives of slaves. Even more than white antiformalists, African American evangelicals believed that the divine voice could come directly.

Among nineteenth-century formal evangelicals, the churches that were most directly the heirs of the Calvinist tradition—the Congregational and the Presbyterian—were strongest in upholding the responsibilities of an educated clergy in biblical interpretation. The Westminster Confession—the most important Calvinist creed—emphatically declared that Scripture had "all things necessary" for human "salvation, faith, and life." The Confession rejected dreams and visions as beyond the Bible, and later Calvinists branded as heretics those who believed God spoke directly to human beings. Other Protestants would not contest the Scripture's primacy in matters of salvation and faith, but Calvinists went further in holding that the Bible provided a sufficient framework for all of life's activities. The corollary was the belief that American society should reflect biblical principles and that the United States would prosper only to the degree it followed scriptural morality.

At the same time, formal evangelicals were committed to having highly educated ministers interpret the Word of God. While stating that "those things which are necessary to be known ... for salvation" were clear to everyone, the Westminster Confession added that "all things in scripture are not alike plain in themselves, nor alike clear to all." Only those who had a grasp of the totality of the Bible were equipped to interpret difficult and obscure passages.

In the late eighteenth and early nineteenth centuries, the formalist commitment to clerical education was reinforced by a philosophical system known as Scottish Common Sense

Realism. According to Common Sense epistemology, truth could be known if humans had access to facts and if they followed the inductive reasoning methods developed by Francis Bacon. Trained ministers had the best access to biblical facts as they could read Scripture in the original Greek and Hebrew, thus bypassing the problems inherent in studying any translation. Well-educated clergy also knew classical history and literature, which helped them understand the Bible by contextualizing difficult passages.

Perhaps the most important advantage of this methodology was how Common Sense theologians could harmonize Scripture with new scientific discoveries in ways that ordinary believers could not. For instance, by the mid-nineteenth century geological discoveries indicated that the earth was far older than the six thousand years suggested by Genesis. Scientifically aware clergymen reconciled the contradiction either by pointing out that the Hebrew word for "day" used in the "six days of creation" could also mean a period of indefinite length, or by arguing that there was an enormous chronological gap between Genesis 1:1, which referred to the original creation of the world, and Genesis 1:2–31, which described the creation of the earth as we know it.

In the 1820s many ministers continued to deliver doctrinal sermons which were modeled after the inductive method. Every sermon was divided into text (the reading of Scripture), exposition (the explanation of Scripture), and proof (the application of Scripture to daily life). Doctrinal sermons had an abundance of evidence and logic but rarely included everyday examples to illustrate points, at least not before the portion dealing with application. On a typical Sunday preachers usually delivered a morning and an afternoon sermon, each address being an hour to an hour and a half.

Although such rigorous, methodical, and abstract preaching retained an appeal for those Northern Presbyterians and Congregationalists who had cut their teeth on a hard-edged and uncompromising Calvinism, even many formalists were uncomfortable with such dry abstraction. While no formalist theologian wished to dispense with the doctrinal sermon, some sought to soften its edges. In the 1820s and 1830s Presbyterian evangelist Charles Grandison Finney advocated storytelling and a conversational preaching style. But even Finney did not move far beyond the intellectual sermon. He had studied law before his conversion to evangelical Christianity, and he delivered his sermons as though he was arguing a case before a jury—including a discussion of the meaning of words in the original Greek to make his point.

Although the doctrinal sermon had been refined, this style of preaching was not significantly challenged until the 1850s. Horace Bushnell,* pastor of the prominent North Congregational Church in Hartford, Connecticut, wanted to reach parishioners "who believed in reform, self-improvement, and gentility, who were nervous and nostalgic about the faith of their fathers, who were affronted by Calvinist accusations and bored by theology." To do so, Bushnell had to move beyond the "dry formalities" of Northern doctrinal preaching. Reasoning that the exuberant emotional preaching of Western revivalism would only offend his middle- to upper-class constituency, Bushnell developed a new approach which emphasized the poetic rather than the doctrinal aspects of the Bible. The good sermon did not follow a rigid, theoreti-

*Scholars are divided on Bushnell's evangelical credentials. William McLoughlin calls Bushnell a Romantic Evangelical, and others refer to Bushnell as a father of liberal Protestantism. Martin Marty combines both points of view by calling Bushnell an evangelical liberal. In any case, his influence on antebellum evangelicalism was great, and he is therefore included in this study.

cal outline but used figurative language, factual examples, and emotional warmth to touch men and women in their everyday lives. The Bushnellian approach became popular with other formalist preachers and eventually became the dominant homiletical style of the late nineteenth century.

Just as the sermon was the focal point of Sunday worship, daily prayer and Bible reading was to be the center of daily life. All evangelicals believed that parents should lead their children in prayer and Bible reading at the beginning and end of every day. As long as families worked together on the family farm, fathers could easily lead daily devotions. The nature of family worship changed with urbanization and the growth of the middle class. Men found it much more difficult to lead the family in daily Bible reading when they left home in the morning and pursued their occupations in a distant workplace. With husbands absent, the task of leading the family in devotions fell to housewives. Despite the shift of religious responsibility from male to female hands, daily prayer and Bible reading were the norm in formal evangelical homes, whether one looks at farm households in 1820 or well-to-do Victorian families in 1860. To assist formalist women with their spiritual responsibilities, Congregational and Presbyterian churches across the Northern states were by the 1830s organizing maternal associations. These societies provided child-rearing information, advice for nurturing children's spirituality, and libraries with "the best books and periodicals which treat the subject of early physical, moral and intellectual education." As one association advocate observed, "How can [the mother's] deficiencies be supplied but *by reading?*"

Formal evangelicals recognized only the Bible, when interpreted by those who were educationally qualified, as the legitimate Word of God. Such evangelicals preferred God's words to be visible, concrete, and on paper, where the formalist clergy would be better equipped than others to understand, interpret, and control the divine message. Given their belief that God spoke only through the written word, formal evangelicals saw it as their duty to spread institutions of literacy which made it possible for common folk to read and understand the Word of God. These believers were also committed to an orderly, productive, and modernizing society and saw themselves, the best-educated evangelicals in the land, as arbiters of the new order. Immorality, in addition to being evil on Christian grounds, brought chaos and disruption and endangered the Republic. As good Christians and true patriots, formal evangelicals sought to bring order to the Republic and salvation and self-discipline to ordinary folk. Accordingly, nineteenth-century formal evangelicals established a wide variety of educational institutions and created a national interdenominational network that distributed Bibles and other religious literature.

The main impetus behind these efforts was alarm over the danger of an ungodly, uncontrolled West. The land beyond the Appalachians appeared to be untutored and uncivilized, and only proper theological and moral teaching could restore order. "The conflict which is to decide the destiny of the West," warned Lyman Beecher, the leading Congregational preacher of his day, in his 1835 essay *A Plea for the West*, "will be a conflict of institutions for the education of her sons, for purposes of superstition, or evangelical light; of despotism, or liberty."

The first step in saving the West was to spread formalist churches throughout the trans-Appalachian region. Accordingly, Presbyterians and Congregationalists combined their efforts to Christianize the West. The Plan of Union of 1801 provided that Presbyterian and Congregational clergy and members could serve or join a congregation of the other denomination without jeopardizing their standing in their home denomination. As a result the distinctions between the two blurred, and "Presbygational" churches were formed in many communities. Nor did Presbyterian and Congregational missionaries compete against each other in the same community. If a Presbygational church was already present, the missionary headed farther west. Formalist attempts to win the frontier received a further boost with the creation of the American Home Missionary Society in 1826. In theory the Home Missionary Society was interdenominational, but in fact it assisted only Presbyterian and Congregational clergymen and refused to aid Baptist, Methodist, or Episcopal ministers.

Yet the insistence on college-educated clergy handicapped Congregational and Presbyterian missionary efforts. By the 1820s New England colleges were producing more than fifteen hundred college-trained ministers each decade, but the supply of clergy still could not keep up with Western demand. Rather than increasing the clerical supply by relaxing standards, formalists chose to enhance their ability to educate ministers by building colleges throughout the Western states. Between 1818 and the Civil War the Presbyterians and Congregationalists created fifty-one colleges, three-fourths of which were located beyond the Appalachians, many of them organized by Princeton and Yale graduates who sought to replicate their alma maters in less settled regions.

Although the primary goal of formalist colleges was to educate ministers, these institutions also sought to civilize and Christianize their student bodies. The denominational college was also a local college and, in many cases, was the only institution of higher education available in a given community. Talented lower- and middle-class students who wanted further education but who could not afford to attend elite Eastern institutions had no choice but to attend the local college. Thus the college became a means to spread formal evangelical culture, which stressed the reasonableness of Christianity, literary awareness, respect for the classics, and deference to those of high educational attainment. In addition to being instruments of order, formalist colleges were instruments of conversion. The vast majority of those attending denominational colleges went for educational, as opposed to religious, reasons. Evangelical faculty members thus saw their student bodies as mission fields, and students were urged to seek salvation either individually or in periodic revivals.

Despite the importance of a college education for ministerial candidates, formalist evangelicals preferred that graduates not go immediately from the college classroom to parish work. Traditionally, prospective clergymen often studied with a senior minister for one to three years after graduation. In the early nineteenth century, formalists realized they could complete ministerial education more efficiently if they established theological seminaries where study could be centralized rather than have apprentices paired with senior ministers across the country. By 1840 Congregationalists had founded five seminaries, the best known being at Yale, Andover, and Oberlin. That same year the Presbyterians had organized seven theological graduate schools, the most notable being Union Seminary in New York City, Lane Seminary in Ohio, and Princeton Seminary in New Jersey. In addition, evangelical Episcopalians had organized Bexley Hall, a theological school connected with Kenyon College, and the German Reformed had established Lancaster Seminary in Pennsylvania.

While educating the elite helped advance their cause, formal evangelicals knew they had to reach the great mass of Americans if they were to Christianize the nation. Thus they advocated four institutions—the public schools and Sunday Schools to promote literacy, and the American Bible Society and the American Tract Society to build on literacy already established.

Formal evangelicals were in the forefront of the movement for public elementary and secondary schools. Frequently, powerful nonevangelical groups, such as the Unitarians, joined in efforts to create strong state-supported educational systems. The alliance across theological lines was possible because, while they disagreed over the nature of God and the divinity of Jesus, Unitarians and orthodox formalists believed in the need for order and centralized authority, in the correctness of traditional American institutions, and in the idea that the Republic could not survive (particularly once all adult white males could vote) unless the citizenry was educated to be responsible and virtuous. Both groups agreed that the children of poor Catholic immigrants were particularly dangerous in that they supposedly lacked habits of frugality and industry, belonged to a foreign, hierarchical, and unrepublican church, and failed to appreciate the American way of life. The answer to these problems was simple—create a public school system that all children would be forced to attend.

The public school movement advanced most quickly in Massachusetts. Beginning in 1830 the American Institute of Instruction (whose members were almost exclusively Congregationalist and Unitarian) pushed for a centralized statewide educational system with a large, standard, and graded curriculum. Reformers also advocated a state normal school for the systematic education of teachers, a school fund to assist poorer localities, and compulsory education so that those most in need of education (poor Catholic children in mill towns) would not escape the benefits of learning. By 1836 the Institute had achieved many of its goals. Perhaps most important, Massachusetts created a state department of education (whose membership was 50 percent clergy) and named Horace Mann, a Unitarian, secretary of the board. Mann used his position to advocate Massachusetts-like school policies in states across the country. As he traveled outside New England, his strongest allies were often formal evangelicals of middle- and upper-class status. For instance, Calvin Stowe and John Pierce, leading reformers in Ohio and Michigan, respectively, were both staunch Congregationalists.

As the reformers saw it, the survival of the Republic depended on the public school's ability to inculcate proper values in every citizen. Since community virtue was the sum total of individual virtue, the best way to insure the Republic's survival was for elementary and secondary schools to teach morality along with the basic skills of reading, writing, and arithmetic. Good citizenship was the end. Conflict arose when it came to defining the source of goodness.

Evangelicals, being inclined toward political activism, frequently dominated both local and state boards of education. In most Northern communities, reading the King James Version of the Bible, reciting the Protestant version of the Lord's Prayer, and studying moralistic textbooks such as William McGuffey's *Eclectic Reader* (120 million copies were sold before 1900) became part of public school routine. Textbooks affirmed that Protestant nations were "more advanced in knowledge" and were "distinguished for justice and kindness," whereas Roman Catholic nations were characterized by "degeneracy and ruin." In response, Catholics in

many communities set up their own parochial school systems
in order to escape Protestant indoctrination. This tactic only
frustrated and angered school reformers, who sought to ban
parochial schools in order to keep their primary targets
within the public school system.

Some Protestant leaders realized that without compulsory
education laws it would be impossible to teach literacy and
Christianity to the poorest children, because these youngsters
had to work during the week to help support their families.
As a result, benevolent reformers created the Sunday School,
which operated on the one day of the week when urban
workplaces were closed. During the 1820s Sunday Schools
spread rapidly. The vast majority were evangelical in out-
look and placed primary emphasis on conversion. At the
same time they promoted order and self-discipline. Along
with requiring memorization of Bible passages, Sunday
Schools encouraged children to "come clean, washed and
combed," and to develop the habit of benevolence by giving
small sums to mission offerings. Similarly, schools rewarded
punctuality and regular attendance with small prizes. The
Benton Street Mission Sunday School in St. Louis listed as
one of its benefits that "it trains the children in the practice of benevolence, love, obedience to parents, truthfulness,
kindness to one another, and purity of language." As one
advocate put it bluntly, "Seven years' good schooling will
cost less than the sheriff's bill for hanging a man."

In 1824 the scattered organizations making up the Sunday
School movement coalesced into a national organization
called the American Sunday School Union. Although the
Union was officially nondenominational, many of its Northern state organizations were dominated by Congregationalists. In the Middle Atlantic and Southern states the movement was controlled primarily by Presbyterians, members of

other Reformed bodies, and Low Church (evangelical) Episcopalians. Once founded, the American Sunday School Union grew at a phenomenal rate. Eight years after its establishment the national body had more than 8,200 affiliates spread across all twenty-four states. Part of the agency's success came from having two very specific goals—to send missionaries to establish new schools in neglected areas, and to furnish existing schools with a wide variety of attractive books, pamphlets, and papers. The missionary efforts met with uneven results, but the publishing activities were highly successful as the national body became a major publisher of children's literature for the remainder of the century.

By controlling American agencies of education, formal evangelicals wielded enormous power and influence. But if American citizens did not have access to wholesome and uplifting literature, efforts at redeeming the Republic through literacy would be in vain. The American Sunday School Union published Christian materials for children, but who would meet the needs of adults? Formal evangelicals founded two agencies, the American Bible Society and the American Tract Society, to publish materials suitable for the general reading public.

From its beginning in 1816, Presbyterians made up a majority of the board of the American Bible Society. To marshal interdenominational support, the Bible Society distributed Bibles "without note or comment," which, in most cases, meant that the King James Version was selected for dissemination. Just as leading common school proponents thought it proper to use public schools to transmit Protestant morality, Bible Society officers thought the government should help in the dissemination of religious literature. In 1817 the Society petitioned Congress for free postage and exemption from duties on the paper used in Bibles. Although it failed to receive this favored treatment, by 1837 the Society had sold and given away 2.2 million Bibles and New Testaments. As of 1846 the organization claimed twelve hundred auxiliaries and was operating even in Central and South America.

The American Tract Society, founded in 1825, was even more successful than the American Bible Society in publishing religious material. This organization first focused on printing four- to twelve-page pamphlets which encouraged readers to be moral and, if poor, to accept poverty as an honorable station in life. By 1828 the Tract Society began to shift its emphasis to evangelism. Its chief concern became the promotion of salvation among the poor. It even employed "tract visitors" to go into destitute urban areas and read tracts to those who could not read for themselves. By 1836 it had published more than 43 million items, primarily tracts but also classics such as John Bunyan's *Pilgrim's Progress*. The 712 million pages printed equaled forty pages of religious material for every man, woman, and child in the United States.

From 1825 to 1841 the Tract Society's publishing committee consisted of a Presbyterian, a Congregationalist, a Low Church Episcopalian, a member of the Dutch Reformed Church, and a Baptist. Only the Baptist came out of an antiformal tradition. Like the American Bible Society, the Tract Society equated its aims with the good of the nation. In 1825 the Society announced its primary goal as "securing and augmenting our civil and political liberties" by molding public opinion through "a moral and religious influence."

These efforts by formal evangelicals to bring salvation and self-discipline to ordinary folk were often rebuffed by those whom they were supposedly trying to help. The largest portion of American evangelicals, the antiformalists, viewed formalist benevolence with deep skepticism. Although believing that God spoke through the Bible, antiformal evangelicals rejected the notion that educated clergy were needed to interpret Scripture for the laity, given the high rate of literacy in the United States.

Like the formalists, antiformal evangelicals were strongly influenced by the Scottish Common Sense Realists. But they were more attracted by Common Sense psychology than by the Baconian inductive method. Unlike Locke, who saw the human mind as a *tabula rasa* or blank slate, Scottish philosophers believed that God installed certain principles within the mind that allowed each person to know what was true and what was false. Closely related to Scottish psychology was the popular notion that God wrote the Bible so it would be easy to understand. Thus the Bible meant exactly what it said, and the best interpretation of God's Word was that which was most literal. A knowledge of the original texts was not required. From the antiformal viewpoint, it was common sense that God would want people to know him through the Word, so seeking him through easy-to-understand modern translations was perfectly acceptable.

The antiformalist notion of having every person become his own biblical interpreter fit the democratic mood of early nineteenth-century America. When circuit rider Peter Cartwright encountered views that disagreed with his Methodist teaching, he "searched the Bible for the true fulfillment of promise and prophecy, prayed to God for light and Divine aid, and proclaimed open war against these delusions." Similarly Abraham Lincoln, who came from a separatist Baptist background, studied the Scriptures independently and used the Bible as a source of strength in times of personal and national crisis. The "Christians" went furthest in advocating personal interpretation. Barton Stone and Alexander Campbell wanted to restore Christendom to a simple apostolic faith free of denominations. They rejected formalist creeds, clergy, and seminaries, and Campbell argued for "the inalienable right of all laymen to examine the sacred writings for themselves."

Antiformal evangelicals agreed with their formalist brethren on the importance of the sermon and concurred that preaching was the high point of worship, had to convey God's message to the audience, and had to provide a vehicle for the Holy Spirit to touch the hearts of sinners. But antiformalists took a very different approach to how sermons should perform these tasks. Unlike most formal evangelicals, Baptists, Methodists, and "Christians" believed effective preaching had to be extemporaneous and emotional, with vigorous gestures. Abraham Lincoln commented that a good preacher should "act as if he were fighting bees." In the South even the Presbyterians gravitated toward antiformalist preaching, though they were still more likely than Baptists or Methodists to write out sermons or use notes. One Southerner looked forward to seeing Presbyterian William Plumer return to the pulpit: "I am hungry to hear him roar once more. I want to see his eyes glare and his hair stand up on end. It will refresh me to see him foam at the mouth again." Good preaching went beyond the intellect and stirred the emotions. Only when hearts were awakened would sinners be saved.

Unlike formal evangelicals, antiformalists believed that God did not restrict himself to the written word but could speak to his children through dreams and visions. Among Baptists a remarkable dream could serve as proof of conversion and often opened the door to baptism and full church membership. Methodist itinerant Lorenzo Dow believed that

God gave him almost constant guidance through the me-
dium of dreams. Visions occasionally were accompanied by
dramatic healing. In 1842 Methodist preacher James Finley
lay near death. After seven days of fevered illness Finley
claimed he was visited by an angel who promised "to
conduct you to another state and place of existence." Finley
was then swept up to "luminous worlds afar...with the
velocity of thought." After touring heaven and seeing a
beautiful child angel, Finley said that "the power of the
eternal God came upon me, and I began to shout, and,
clapping my hands, I sprang from my bed, and was healed
...instantly." The only limit antiformalists placed on dreams
and visions was that they not contradict Scripture.

Lower-class whites of the West and South, who formed
the backbone of antiformal evangelical churches, believed
that God spoke to them through the Bible which could be
interpreted literally, through preachers who relied on the
Holy Spirit rather than on human intellect, and through
dreams and visions. With these God-given gifts, antiformalists sought to free themselves from two vestiges of the
aristocratic past—creed and clergy. Antiformalists were particularly incensed over the Westminster Confession, the theological foundation of Calvinism, the religion of the formalist
elite.

Viewing creeds as instruments used by theological elites to
impose their ideas on those who were less educated, antiformal evangelicals dismissed the Westminster Confession by
appealing to a higher power—the Bible itself. "No creed but
the Bible" became the rallying cry.

An educated professional clergy was also seen as a threat,
since the rich and powerful used their superior access to
education to monopolize biblical interpretation. Fancy degrees corrupted true spirituality for, as Cartwright put it,

"educational pride has been the downfall and ruin of many preeminently educated ministers of the Gospel."

Antiformalists generally believed that the only clerical qualifications were that a man had been converted and had received a "call" direct from God to preach. Ministers were not to be wealthy, well educated, or an agent of some outside (and uncontrollable) ecclesiastical power.

Antiformal evangelicals distrusted mission agencies because such organizations appeared to support the wrong kind of clergy: men who were salaried, often educated, and who took instructions from distant headquarters which made them independent of local control. The American Home Missionary Society was a major concern. Many antiformalists were afraid that this powerful outside agency, controlled by Eastern elites, would destroy freedom of worship and local congregational autonomy.

So it was that most antiformalists refused to cooperate with the AHMS and instead pursued missionary work under denominational auspices. In 1814 Baptists organized their own national agency, the Baptist General Missionary Conference. The Methodist church, by comparison, was already a huge missionary organization, as an army of circuit riders spread out into the remotest frontier regions. But by 1830 the Methodists supplemented their system with national support agencies. "Christians" in New England created their own missionary organization in the 1830s. In 1849 even Alexander Campbell reversed his earlier opposition to missionary agencies and the Disciples formed the American Christian Missionary Society.

Not all antiformalists believed that missionary agencies were safe when placed under denominational control: some opposed *all* outside organizations on principle. Those who battled even their own denomination's agencies were the

most marginalized whites. As the historian Bertram Wyatt-
Brown pointed out, "the antimissionists were primarily a
rural, economically insecure people" in "the antebellum
South" and "northern agrarian communities as well."

Much antimission sentiment was based on a Jefferson-
Jacksonian fear of powerful, elitist, Eastern-based national
institutions. Opposition to the so-called Monster Bank of the
United States and to "bloodsucking" mission organizations
had the same source—a fear of being consumed by well-
educated, elite Northerners. Southern and Western farmers
and craftsmen were annoyed by constant requests for contri-
butions. In North Carolina a Baptist pamphlet, *The American Telescope,* condemned mission advocates, saying, "These
beggars are like hungry mosquitoes—knock them off, and
they will be at you again, and again, until they suck your
money if possible." When denominational agencies spent
disproportionate sums on work in the North, Southern
suspicion about the "benevolent" nature of the agencies was
confirmed. Rather than give money to much distant nefari-
ous groups, those who had political and economic objections
argued that the congregation was the only religious institution mentioned in the Bible, and therefore it was the only
institution God had sanctioned for the salvation of souls.
Thus local control and biblical literalism both served the
antimission cause.

Like missionary work, the foundation of colleges and
seminaries was a controversial issue in antebellum America.
Many antiformalists rejected outright efforts to start denominational colleges. Formal education had always been the
enemy, whether it enabled an elite laity to laugh at the rustic
manners of Southern and Western farmers or empowered
elite clergy to claim they alone could interpret the Word of
God. The antiformalists who opposed colleges believed that

structured self-education was all ministers needed. Because "God never called an unprepared man to preach," minimal instruction was all that was deemed necessary. Baptists used the "solitary" method in which one or two ministerial candidates lived with an established pastor who tutored them and allowed them to use his personal library; in turn they assisted him with his clerical duties. Essentially the younger men were ministerial apprentices. By using this method, Baptists perpetuated a system of instruction that was dying out in other lines of work. Methodists developed the Course of Study. In this system each candidate studied a series of doctrinal works, commentaries, sermons, and biographies that were recommended by the General Conference. After two years of self-directed study (in 1844 the time was expanded to four years) the prospective preacher was examined on his knowledge of Scripture and Methodist doctrine.

Other antiformalists accepted a need for higher education. Some were afraid that the Presbyterian and Congregational colleges being established throughout the West would corrupt their denomination's best and brightest. The religious revivals that swept many colleges in the 1820s and 1830s dampened the suspicion of colleges. A drive for respectability also pushed antiformalists in the direction of higher education. Baptists were generally the most prosperous antiformalists, and nowhere were Baptists better off than in New England, where they rubbed shoulders with affluent Congregationalists and Unitarians and thereby picked up elite ideas. By the 1820s New England Baptists were arguing for an educated ministry because church members demanded more literate sermons and because learned preachers were necessary if Baptists were to reach the educated and cultivated people in society.

In 1820 the Baptists had one college (Brown University in

Rhode Island) and the Methodists and "Christians" had none. By 1830 three more Baptist and two Methodist institutions were founded. The next thirty years saw an antiformal building boom. By 1861 the Methodists had thirty-four colleges, the Baptists twenty-five, and the Disciples six. In terms of sheer numbers the antiformalists had nearly caught up, but in terms of providing education for their young people, they still lagged behind. In 1860 the Presbygationalists had one college for every twelve thousand members; the Methodists and Baptists had one college for every fifty thousand members.

Although enthusiasm for colleges led to formalist seminaries, traditional opposition to an educated clergy stifled any similar movement among antiformal evangelicals. Traditionalists agreed with the *Christian Advocate*'s 1840 declaration that "all history shows that the Church invariably declines in spirituality in the same proportion as her ministers become distinguished for their general popularity as eloquent and learned divines." Before 1859 antiformal theological seminaries were established only in the Northeast. Baptists established Colgate Seminary in New York State in 1817 and Newton Seminary in Massachusetts in 1824. Methodists opened a theological institution in Vermont in 1839. But the Methodist opposition to seminaries remained so vigorous that its founder dared not use the term; hence the new institution was designated the Newbury Biblical Institute. Disciples of Christ leader Alexander Campbell supported the denomination's Bethany College only as long as the school had no professorship in theology. Overall most antiformalists modified their opposition to higher education, but their disdain for cultivated, urbane ministers remained strong.

Antiformalists supported the public school movement in

principle but were wary of elite Protestant manipulation of
the curriculum. Lower-class white evangelicals looked upon
education as a means of advancement, not a badge of elite
privilege. Reading, writing, and arithmetic were necessary
for personal advancement and self-improvement. Let the
state provide the basics and an industrious citizen could gain
the rest of his education on his own initiative. Antiformalists
thus usually did not oppose common school education unless
formalists attempted to include Presbygational teaching in
the curriculum. Typically, evangelicals managed to agree on
a lowest-common-denominator Protestantism which trans-
cended denominational boundaries. Bible-reading, the (Protestant) Lord's Prayer, the Ten Commandments, and moral
instruction were acceptable to antiformalists as long as overt
sectarianism was absent.

While antiformalists generally accepted public education,
they were divided over Sunday Schools. Whereas formalists
supported a highly organized, national program under the
American Sunday School Union, "Christian" leaders like
Alexander Campbell opposed the national agency from the
start. Methodists cooperated with the American Sunday
School Union until 1827. But when the ASSU tilted in a
Calvinist direction and considered publishing public school
textbooks, many Methodists were alarmed. The Methodists
drew on their own tradition of Sabbath instruction dating
back to the eighteenth century, broke from the national
agency to establish the Methodist Sunday School Union, and
used only the teaching materials published by the Methodist
Book Concern.

Unlike the Methodists, the Baptists did not move quickly
to establish a national rival to the American Sunday School
Union. Northern urban Baptists, who had growing formalist
tendencies, worked comfortably with the Union. Other Bap-

tists, particularly those in the rural South, were highly suspicious of the Sunday School movement. As missionary James E. Welch noted, lower-class Southern whites "think . . . that a Sunday school is too much like teaching blacks on Sunday while some of the poor are offended at it as too much like singling them out from their richer neighbors."

Antiformalists agreed that having solid, edifying reading material was important. Literacy, in the absence of evangelical books and pamphlets, only opened the believer to a wider range of temptations. All evangelicals believed the most important book was the Bible, and the American Bible Society, which distributed the King James Version without note or comment, received broad antiformalist support. Even Alexander Campbell reversed his usual antiformalist stance by becoming a life director of the American Bible Society. Only the Old School Baptists remained hostile. They were so petrified of the Northeastern religious elite and their well-heeled Southern counterparts that they did the opposite of whatever the formal evangelicals did. Describing the Bible Society as "a monstrous combination, concentrating so much power in the hands of a few individuals," the Old School Baptists argued that individuals alone could distribute Bibles more effectively.

If evangelicals reached consensus on Bible distribution, they were badly divided over the dissemination of other religious literature. The American Tract Society materials were written from a Calvinist perspective, which made them unacceptable to most antiformalists. So antiformal evangelicals competed against formal evangelical agencies for the religious reading public. The Methodist Book Concern began denominational publishing in 1789, and in the 1820s it moved beyond books into printing magazines, children's literature, biblical commentaries, and a scholarly journal.

Methodists also launched into the newspaper business by publishing the *Christian Advocate and Journal*, which had the largest circulation of any newspaper in the world by 1829. Alexander Campbell established a press that disseminated Disciples of Christ literature. Old School Baptists attacked tract societies, arguing that distributing such literature led to the neglect of the Bible and to a decline in religious knowledge. But Old School partisans had no objection to printing their views through periodicals such as the *Reformer* and *Signs of the Times*. In general, antiformalists had no objection to the widespread dissemination of religious litera-ture as long as it was written and published under denom-inational auspices.

Like white evangelicals, African American evangelicals con-sidered the Bible to be the authoritative and divinely in-spired Word of God. But God did not speak in a vacuum. Readers always approached the Bible with their own as-sumptions and cultural expectations. Just as formalists brought education to the interpretative process, and antifor-malists examined Scripture through the lens of common sense, African American evangelicals understood Scripture in light of evangelical teaching, African tradition, and the slave experience. White missionaries conveyed essential evan-gelical ideas in their efforts to convert the slaves, but African American believers reworked those ideas in light of African custom and the experience of slavery. While Africans sel-dom communicated with the creator or High God, they con-stantly interacted with ancestral and other spirits. Black evangelicals also saw God as being exceptionally close. "Many of the blacks," one white preacher observed, "look upon white people as merely taught by the Book; they consider themselves instructed by the inspiration of the Spirit."

In Africa, to verbalize was to make real (in some tribes, those who described an act of adultery in a dream were punished as harshly as those who actually committed the act). Thus the Word of God became most real in its oral forms—in preaching and in spirituals. West African oral tradition emphasized communal storytelling as heroic deeds were recreated in the present. Similarly, African American sermons focused on Old Testament narratives and stories about Jesus. The slave experience influenced the choice of stories as the most popular texts were accounts of divine deliverance.

African American evangelicals believed that the Bible, if interpreted properly with the guidance of the Holy Spirit, was a reliable guide for both the present and the hereafter. Like other evangelicals, African Americans most frequently heard the Word of God in the sermon. But sermons were articulated in three contexts. White ministers could preach to blacks, black preachers and exhorters could speak with whites present, or blacks could minister to each other in the absence of whites.

White pastors ministered to a large number of integrated and all-black churches throughout the South. Many African American Baptists and Methodists were members of integrated churches. But they generally sat in segregated seating, received the sacraments last, and were not given equal access to burial in church cemeteries. Thus African Americans sought to form separate all-black congregations whenever possible. Baptists organized all-black fellowships more quickly than Methodists, and separate African Baptist congregations flourished in many urban areas.

Blacks most frequently heard white sermons in the plan-

tation mission. Many white evangelicals sought to Christianize the slaves by preaching to bondservants where they
worked and lived. Slaveholders were afraid that Christianity's message of spiritual equality would make slaves rebel-
lious, so mission advocates countered by arguing that, once
Christianized, slaves would be more docile and easily controlled. By the 1830s white evangelists developed a second
argument in support of mission activity. Northern abolitionists were attacking slavery on the grounds that slaveholders
kept blacks from religious instruction. So mission supporters
argued that by permitting religious instruction, planters
could effectively refute antislavery propaganda. The mission
efforts of both Southern Methodists and Southern Baptists
apparently met with some success as both claimed to double
their black memberships between 1845 and 1861.

Whether they were listening to urban ministers or to a
rural plantation missionary, African American evangelicals
were usually uninspired by white preaching. Some formalists tried to use methods that were totally inappropriate. One
young minister began a doctrinalist sermon with the pro-
nouncement, "Primarily, we must postulate the existence of a
deity," to which an elderly black man responded, "Yes, Lord,
dat's so. Bless de Lord." Another tried to teach slaves to sing
in Latin. More important than cultural differences was the
fact that white preachers had compromised their credibility
by selling out to slavery. By the 1830s white Baptist and
Methodist clergy no longer openly opposed slavery. The
message of slave obedience alienated black listeners who
were too often told, "Don't you tell lies. Don't you steal."
Virginia's Nancy Williams represented the sentiments of
many when she said, "Dat ole white preachin' wasn't nothin'. Ole white preachers used to talk wid dey tongues

widdout sayin' nothin' but Jesus told us slaves to talk wid our hearts."

Black evangelicals preferred their own preachers. After 1831, however, Southern state laws curtailed the number of licensed free black and slave preachers and required that white slaveholders be present at all black worship services. With whites present, black preachers had to echo the "servants obey your masters" theme. Ex-slave Charlie van Dyke revealed: "Church was what they called it but all that preacher talked about was for us slaves to obey our masters and not to lie and steal. Nothing about Jesus was ever said and the overseer stood there to see the preacher talked as he wanted him to talk." Another former slave confessed that he had to preach the planter message, to "tell them niggers iffen they obeys the massa they goes to heaven." Only when all whites were absent could he speak his heart: "iffen they keeps prayin' the Lord will set 'em free."

There were two places where antebellum black evangelicals could speak what they believed was God's Word free from white interference. The first was in Northern black congregations. By the early 1820s black Methodists had organized two denominations, both of which grew out of a desire for independence after white-appointed supervisors interfered with congregational decisions. In 1816 Richard Allen spearheaded the formation of the African Methodist Episcopal Church. Six years later James Varick became bishop of a second group that would eventually be known as the African Methodist Episcopal Zion Church. Both denominations adhered to Methodist theology, added a much stronger denunciation of slavery to their *Discipline*, and included African elements in preaching and worship. At the same time African Americans formed black Baptist congregations in cities like Boston, New York, and Philadelphia. Because all

Baptist churches were autonomous, black Baptists were free from white interference and saw no immediate need to create a new denomination. They too denounced the peculiar institution and included African cultural patterns in Christian worship.

The second place where blacks preached the Word of God was in the Southern hush harbors—secret meeting places where slaves could worship free from white supervision. Some masters forbade missions or religious services of any kind; others permitted Sunday worship but would not allow after-hours worship during the week. Many whites so constrained black religious sentiment that slaves' deepest spiritual desires went unexpressed. As a result, many devout slaves "stole away to Jesus" by meeting secretly in the woods where they could speak and worship God free from white interference. Great personal risk accompanied the secret meetings. Slaves caught at illicit prayer meetings were generally flogged. David Walker stated that many of those beaten for attending hush harbor meetings "would hardly be able to crawl for weeks and sometimes for months." Charlotte Martin claimed "her oldest brother was whipped to death for taking part in one of the religious ceremonies."

Like other evangelicals, African American believers placed great authority in the hands of the preacher who was obligated to deliver sermons based on the Bible. Part of the preacher's authority came from African tradition. In the old country, leaders combined the religious functions of the priest, who mediated with ancestral and other spirits, with those of the king, who led the community. When slaves became Christians, the role of priest-king fell to the preacher who spoke the Scripture and interpreted Holy Writ for the community. Free black and slave preachers could usually read and write, thus making them among the very few Southern blacks who could interpret the Bible for themselves.

Literacy, however, was not an essential requirement for ministry. Like many in preliterate cultures, African American bondsmen had amazing skills of memorization. Black revivalist John Jasper was reputed to have committed most of the Bible to memory. The most important ministerial requirement was "having the spirit," for "it is God in the soul, that makes the religious teacher." An exhorter named Uncle Link had the gift even though "he couldn't read the scriptures." But all one had to do was to read the Scripture to him and Uncle Link was ready to preach. "He wouldn't talk long before the spirit would strike him and then it was easy sailing. It looked like his very soul would catch on fire."

Having the spirit was essential, but not sufficient: a good black sermon had to be based on Scripture. Unlike white evangelicals who focused on a single text, African Americans gravitated toward stories in the Old Testament and the Gospels. This emphasis on narrative within black sermons was a carryover from the African past. Leaders often entertained the community by recounting the exploits of tribal ancestors. When African Americans became evangelical Protestants, storyteller-ministers kept the emphasis on narrative and celebrated the heroic deeds of the group's spiritual ancestors (Moses, David, Daniel, Jesus, and others). Everyday African folktales, such as the trickster tales in which small animals outwitted their stronger foes, were used to instruct the young. African American sermons conveyed moral instruction using the same techniques. Birds, animals, and common tools were all used to illustrate ideas. With biblical narratives being the foundation of black preaching and everyday objects illustrating moral principles, the African American minister had powerful tools which built on African storytelling to touch the hearts of his listeners.

The experience of slavery heavily influenced which biblical stories appeared in black sermons. African American evangelicals were drawn to God's deliverance of the children of Israel from the hand of Pharoah. Moses captured their imagination as did no other biblical figure. Other stories of divine deliverance and supernatural assistance were popular. Daniel's deliverance from the lion's den, David's defeat of Goliath, Joshua's victory at Jericho confirmed, much as had the trickster tales, that the weak could overcome the strong. And the aspect of Jesus that most fired the black imagination was Jesus' future role as warrior-king, when the Messiah would destroy the enemies of God's people and deliver his children from bondage.

The Word of God expressed in preaching was vitally important; but it was incomplete unless it brought a response from the community. Unlike most white services, black worship had to include audible responses from the listeners. Typically the preacher began speaking in a style not that different from white oratory, but as he developed his central theme from the story, his delivery became rhythmical and intense. As he moved to application, where the truths of the sermon were connected to the needs of the audience, the preacher's words were interrupted by his own grunts and cries. At the same time his listeners would shout out, "Amen!" "Say it again, brother!" "Hallelujah!" "Praise God!" Soon a rhythmic pattern commenced in which the preacher communicated ideas in short bursts and the audience shouted exclamations in unison. As he moved toward the climax, the preacher began to chant, and eventually he or a member of the congregation burst into song. This call-and-response pattern may have originated with storytelling in Africa. Scholars have found that a similar form of listener response existed in secular African American storytelling.

Just as African storytelling was accompanied by dance, so

was the African American evangelical sermon. In Africa, dances moved counterclockwise around the storyteller as he told tales of tribal heroes. Africans used dance to pray to and honor the ancestors by reenacting their famous deeds. The black preacher-storyteller evoked a similar response known as the ring shout. If a preacher was successful in relating the Word of God, his listeners moved beyond call-and-response and began to move rhythmically, in a counterclockwise circle. Meanwhile, those not in the ring would sing a song, tapping their feet and clapping their hands. A single song or spiritual could sustain the ring shout for twenty to thirty minutes. Musicologist Eileen Southern has noted that shouters used the dance to communicate with God and believed they "reached the highest level of worship when the Holy Spirit entered their bodies and took possession of their souls."

The Word of God was expressed in ways other than sermons. For instance, spirituals, which often rose in response to the sermon and provided the music to which the ring shout was performed, recreated biblical events and brought them into the present. Through song, Joshua, Moses, Mary, and Jesus could be emotionally and dramatically present. The battle of Jericho could be refought or Ezekiel's dry bones would again come to life. Songs of solace and redemption were common. Frequently the songs spoke not only about blacks' hopes for the new world but informed about this world as well. Harriet Tubman often used spirituals to convey information about an upcoming escape. "Heaven" could refer to freedom, the "devil" to slaveowners, the "Jordan River" to the Ohio River, and the "sweet chariot" to the underground railroad.

Like white antiformalists, African American evangelicals believed God could guide them directly through inner

promptings, dreams, and visions. Having been denied the
right to read the Bible for themselves (90 percent of all adult
blacks were illiterate in 1865), African American evangelicals believed that God compensated by speaking to them
directly. One ex-slave confidently proclaimed, "Our God
talks to his children." Most often, Jesus spoke to black
believers through an inner voice that touched them in their
hearts. As one female ex-slave said, "Oh! I don't know
nothing! I can't read a word. But oh! I read Jesus in my
heart, just as you read him in de book." Sometimes God
communicated in a more dramatic fashion. One woman
claimed that after her conversion she was "always fore-
warned of trouble." She then related how her recently dead
son appeared to her soon after his death and how she "saw
myself sailing along in mid-air one day" not long after God
told her she would recover from illness.

Yet among black evangelicals there was an overwhelming
desire to receive the Word of God in the same way that most
white folks received it—through the written word. When
Northern whites visited the South during and immediately
after the Civil War, they were struck by the freedman's
"greed for letters." African Americans' postbellum appetite
for literacy drew on a religious motivation—the desire to
study Scripture for themselves. One black minister addressed his flock holding his Bible high above the congregation and said, "Breddern and sisters! I can't read mor'n a
werse or two of dis bressed Book, but de gospel it is
here—de glad tidings it is here—oh teach your chill'en to
read dis yar bressed Book. It's de good news for we poor
coloured folk." An ex-slave from North Carolina expressed
similar desires when he remarked, "If I could on'y read God's
own write I tink it would be wurf more'n than everything."

Even in the North, African American evangelicals faced

significant obstacles to education. Public elementary and secondary schools were segregated by the 1830s and in most communities were still segregated in 1860. Black students were generally sent to dilapidated buildings, had few textbooks, and were taught by indifferent teachers who were convinced that African American intellects were "incapable of being cultured beyond a particular point." The door to Northern black higher education opened slightly in the antebellum period. The first step was admission to white colleges. In the 1820s Alexander Twilight of Middlebury, Edward Jones of Amherst, and John Russwurm of Bowdoin became the nation's first black college graduates. Dartmouth, Western Reserve, and Oberlin also admitted black scholars in the 1820s and 1830s. By the Civil War twenty-eight African Americans had graduated from recognized white colleges, and many more were attending colleges and medical schools. While the number of college graduates was small, the influence on black evangelicalism by those who graduated was great, as many, including Samuel Ringgold Ward, Henry Highland Garnet, and Daniel Alexander Payne, became prominent ministers.

African American leaders and whites sympathetic to their cause both realized that while white colleges would instruct a small number of black scholars, African Americans would not be educated in large numbers until they had colleges of their own. Three of the four black colleges founded before 1860 had evangelical origins. In 1843 the Institute for Colored Youth was incorporated in Philadelphia. Six years later the Reverend Charles Avery provided $25,000 that led to the formation of Avery College in Pennsylvania. In the mid-1850s the Presbyterians formed Ashmun Institute (later Lincoln University), and the Methodists created Wilberforce University. In the early 1860s the African Methodist Episco-

pal Church assumed control of Wilberforce, making it the first
college affiliated with an African American denomination.

The shared emphasis by evangelicals upon the Bible as the
Word of God, and their zeal to preach the Word, would
have a profound influence on American culture. America's
educational infrastructure was largely a by-product of evangelical zeal. About two-thirds of American colleges were
sponsored by evangelical denominations in 1860. The public
school system's most vocal advocates were formal evangelicals and their Unitarian allies.

Evangelicals were also pioneers in mass media. Formalists, in particular, were anxious to use the latest improvements in printing technology to spread the gospel to every
man, woman, and child in the United States. The American
Bible Society and the American Tract Society were the first
major consumers of a new printing process called stereotyp-
ing, which drastically reduced typesetting costs. They were
also the first major users of the steam-powered press and the
chief customers of Amos Hubbard's innovative machine-
papermaking enterprise. By using the latest technology, the
ABS and ATS cut their per-unit publishing costs almost in
half between 1821 and 1831. Antiformalists copied their
methods, as the Methodists used new techniques in their
Book Concern and in printing the *Christian Advocate*. With
advances in print technology, American religious publishing
grew from fourteen newspapers in 1790 to more than six
hundred in 1830. Reformers quickly copied evangelical publishing methods. The American Temperance Society flooded
the nation with antialcohol tracts and the American Anti-
Slavery Society used the same technology in producing
abolitionist literature during the 1830s. By creating a market
for new technology and by demonstrating the cost effective-

ness of new printing methods, the Bible and Tract societies also paved the way for the "penny press." When secular newspapers adopted the techniques pioneered by evangelicals, the American public moved closer to being a "reading public."

Evangelicals created the first national organizations that were fully integrated from the national to the local level. These religious agencies were unique in that they had executive boards creating policy which local agents and auxiliaries then implemented in communities throughout the country. The enormous expansion of Methodism can be attributed to its ecclesiastical structure in which bishops assigned circuit riders (or agents) to organize class meetings across the country. In time the circuit riders would double as colporteurs, or book dealers, for the Methodist Book Concern. The Bible and Tract societies refined this system by creating a board of directors to make policy and by sending out agents to establish local chapters and auxiliaries to implement policy. By 1829 the ABS had 645 local branches and the ATS had 713 auxiliaries.

Not only did temperance and antislavery societies successfully copy evangelical methods, the political process was fundamentally changed by the evangelicals' organizational innovations. In the 1820s party politics were still largely controlled by congressional caucuses which chose presidential candidates and determined party policy. By the late 1820s, however, many citizens were suspicious of elite institutions and demanded a more active role in government. This demand could be met only by creating new institutions; the new political organizers copied many ideas from evangelical Protestantism. The Anti-Masonic party, which included many evangelicals in its campaign against secret societies, organized the first political conventions. The Democrats and the Whigs copied the convention strategy. These national meetings were essentially secular revival meetings where a presidential candidate was chosen, party doctrine was written, and ecstatic party members pledged themselves to the campaign. After the convention local parties (or auxiliaries) supported the national party's platform much as local auxiliaries carried out the goals of the Bible and Tract societies. By the late 1830s the United States had its first modern political parties that were integrated from the national to the local level.

While formalists made their mark on American culture through their organizations, antiformalists influenced the nation by emphasizing literalism. Antiformalists viewed the Bible as a "plain book" that could be easily understood by all. But the tendency to interpret the Bible "word for word" grew stronger as Southern antiformalists realized that a literal interpretation of Scripture could justify slavery. Biblical literalism paralleled political developments as John C. Calhoun and other Southern Democrats argued for a literal or strict construction of the United States Constitution. Literalism thus served slavery in the realm of both biblical interpretation and constitutional law.

African American understandings of the Word also enriched national culture. Blacks realized that the Word not only could be spoken, it could be sung. Group singing about the grace of God and the promise of future redemption sustained many slaves in their daily labor. Many spirituals were recorded and have enriched America's musical heritage. And the communal call-and-response interaction in conjunction with the preaching of the Word led to distinctive African American oratory. This powerful speaking style, which emphasized short sentence structure, memorable phrases, and powerful imagery, has empowered black orators from Frederick Douglass to Martin Luther King, Jr., and Jesse Jackson.

2

The Second Birth

THE PREACHING OF the Word was central to the lives of nineteenth-century evangelicals. But this preaching had a greater purpose—to encourage individuals to seek God and experience the Second Birth. Like most Protestants, evangelicals believed in the Reformation principle of *Sola Fides*, or justification by faith alone. This doctrine viewed human beings as inherently sinful and incapable of earning their way to heaven through good works. God, being just, was obligated to punish those who violated his holy law. Fortunately, for humankind, God mercifully sent his son in the form of a human, Jesus Christ, to live a perfect life and then to die by crucifixion as a substitute for sinful humanity. Humans who had faith in Jesus Christ (i.e., who gave up all attempts to save themselves by doing good works, repented of their wrongdoing, and placed all hope for salvation on Christ's atonement for their sins) would receive eternal life after their earthly sojourn had ended. Although Martin Luther was most responsible for bringing the principle of *Sola Fides* to modern Christianity, evangelicals gave the Lutheran principle of justification by faith a subtle shift in emphasis. Evangelicals contended that true faith was more than belief or trust and required a life-changing experience coming from God himself.

The process of religious conversion followed a distinct pattern. Evangelicals went through a five-step process as they moved from unbelief to a full-fledged member of a Christian community. In the first stage of conversion—conviction—souls were awakened to their sinful condition. In the second stage—struggle—anguished seekers tentatively turned to God as an escape from eternal doom. These attempts at salvation were faltering and inconclusive. Frequently individuals confessed sins, only to repeat them later. By the end of the second stage, most seekers were in a state of despair as the old self sought to maintain itself and a new self struggled to be born.

In the third stage—conversion—convicted sinners finally gave up trying to save themselves. Instead they abandoned themselves to the mercy of God, accepted Christ's death as full pardon for their sins, and in the process received emotional reassurance that God included them among the redeemed. In the nineteenth century the type of internal release that came varied widely. Some testified to experiencing a deep, penetrating sense of peace; others claimed to see Jesus, or to being bathed in light. Outside behavior also varied greatly. In some circles converts were "struck down by the power of God" and laid perfectly still on the ground. Others shouted, yelped, or danced as they were "seized by the Spirit."

In the fourth stage—recognition—converts came to grips with the newness of their lives. Many of the redeemed professed to have new hands and new feet; others claimed new powers. Those who had been plagued by unfortunate habits occasionally related that God had destroyed the appeal of vices that previously had tempted them. In the final stage—reintegration—the life of the convert began to coalesce around the new, revitalized evangelical personality. The initial step into the evangelical life-style usually was formal church membership, which included participation in the two Protestant sacraments—baptism, if they had not been baptized as children, and Communion (or the Lord's Supper).

While evangelicals agreed on the necessity of the Second Birth, social location affected how particular groups perceived and experienced this pivotal event. Although the five-step pattern was common to formal, antiformal, and black evangelicals, the farther a group was from the center of society, the more dramatic and tumultuous were its conversion experiences.

Calvinism influenced formalist theories of conversion. Because God was all-powerful and humans were hopelessly flawed, there was nothing people could do to bring about their own salvation. If redemption was to occur, it would happen only by the grace of God.

By the early nineteenth century traditional Calvinists developed a method by which people could, in a limited way, seek their own conversion. The strategy was to "wait upon the Lord," a wise decision in light of conversion being exclusively in the divine realm. While one waited, some useful activities were possible. Many prayed for divine intervention in their souls. Others read the Bible. Some even wrote extensive diaries as they sought to understand the ways of God. Eventually, however, such exercises led to intense frustration and a sense of helplessness. Although they were ready for God's intervention in their lives, only when they knew they could do nothing and were totally dependent upon God's mercy would God act.

The accompanying transformation experienced by traditional Calvinists was remarkably quiet. The entire personality, both mind and emotions, was reorganized around God's

divine and eternal plan as the convert internalized the
Calvinist understanding of the Christian faith. No longer
did the individual question the nature of God or the justice
of his laws. Instead the affections focused on God, the soul
sought greater understanding, and the self submitted to
divine authority. After conversion, new believers fit themselves into the religious social order. Formal evangelicals
believed that only "visible saints," those fortunate enough to
experience God's intervention in their lives, should be granted full church membership. Thus the first step for new
believers was to testify to their conversion before the church
so that they could receive full membership. The focus of the
testimony and interrogation that followed was not on the
experience of conversion but on doctrine. The truly converted would be able to discuss correctly all points of faith.

By the 1820s the so-called "New School" theologians, led
by Nathaniel Taylor, Lyman Beecher, and Charles Finney,
found the traditionalist formula inadequate. Waiting for
conversion seemed antiquated in an activist, democratic
America. White Americans were free to choose their occu-
pation, their residence, and their social relationships. With
the coming of universal white manhood suffrage, adult
white males involved themselves in politics as never before. Everywhere self-determination beckoned, at least until
one entered a Calvinist church. There parishioners had no
choice, no control over their salvation, but were forced to
wait for a distant, omnipotent God to determine their fate.
The common frustration over election was revealed in a
popular song:

> You can and you can't,
> You shall and you shan't;
> You will and you won't.

You're damned if you do,
And damned if you don't.

The New School theologians reworked formalist theology to bring it in line with a society that held personal freedom and self-determination in high esteem. A professor of theology at the Yale Divinity School, Nathaniel Taylor began the modification of Calvinism with the New Haven Theology. By arguing that mankind had the moral ability to choose good or evil, Taylor shifted the source of human sinfulness from a divine plan to the human will. The problem was not that people could not obey God, according to Taylor, but that "Man will not do what he can do." This being the case, the role of the minister was to appeal to the heart so that sinners would choose the salvation freely offered by Jesus Christ.

While Lyman Beecher spread the New Haven Theology throughout New England, Presbyterian evangelist Charles Finney went even further in reshaping traditional Calvinism. Whereas the New Haven theologians sought to save Calvinism by supporting qualified free will, Finney abandoned Calvinism and adapted Methodist techniques and doctrine to a formalist audience. In accepting the Methodist position that humans were free to accept the grace of God, Finney discarded the doctrine of election altogether. Finney believed that human beings, not God, had the final word on whether they would spend eternity in heaven or hell. In portraying this decision for his audiences, Finney used the most powerful democratic imagery at his disposal—the American political election. "The world is divided into two great political parties," Finney argued. "The difference between them is that one party choose Satan as the god of this world [and] the other party choose Jehovah for their governor." Each individual had a choice, and salvation came when

sinners decided to yield their lives to God, thus joining
Jehovah's party. Election still was a key term in the language
of conversion; but in Finney's view, individual sinners, not
God, cast the crucial ballot which determined salvation or
damnation.

Finney realized that the key to conversion was forcing
his audience to choose, which meant overcoming the tendency of many to defer the decision. The sermon, he believed,
was the key to mass evangelism. He argued, "We must have
exciting, powerful preaching, or the devil will have the
people, except what the Methodists can save." Getting effective preaching meant discarding traditional Presbyterian
conventions such as writing out sermons according to laws of
classical rhetoric and using illustrations from ancient history.
Instead Finney, who was a lawyer before his religious
conversion, delivered his sermons as though he was arguing
a case before a jury. He used everyday examples to illustrate
his point, used "you" when speaking of sinners rather than
the more abstract and less offensive "they," and spoke
extemporaneously, using gestures to increase the emotional
power of his presentation. When he described the fall of
sinners, for example, he pointed to the ceiling, and as his
finger dropped downward, people in the rear seats stood up
so they could see the final entry into the flames of damnation.

But powerful sermons alone could not bring fence-strad-
dlers to the point of decision: Finney used a number of New
Measures to create an environment that would maximize the
beneficial effects of good preaching. The central element of
the New Measures was the "protracted meeting." In western
New York protracted meetings were held for three or four
days at the beginning or end of a series of revival meetings.
During that time pious businessmen, craftsmen, and farmers

and their families would stop their everyday activities and attend dawn-till-dusk religious services at the local church. In the Eastern cities, asking businesses to suspend operations was out of the question, so the protracted meeting was extended to three- or four-week series of nightly meetings. Inevitably the curious, scoffers, and the religiously uncommitted went to the revival services. Once they were within the church walls, Finney was able to spin his magic. The beauty of the protracted meeting was that should a sinner delay deciding for Christ one night, Finney could urge that soul to choose Jesus on a later evening.

Numerous other New Measures were employed within each revival meeting. Many Christians spent the entire time during services in a separate room where they prayed for the salvation of souls, sometimes out loud and by name. Popular religious music was used to set the mood early in the service. At the end of the revival meeting Finney invited those concerned about their souls to come forward to sit on the "anxious seat," usually the front benches or pews, where they could be spoken to or prayed for individually. Altogether the combination of emotional music, powerful sermons, the anxious seat, the inquiry room, extended prayer meetings, and personal testimonies all extended over a period of days or weeks brought the desired impact for Finney and formalists who copied his methods: thousands were converted and joined Presbyterian, Congregational, and evangelical Episcopalian churches.

Finney and evangelists who used similar methods not only made religious conversion immediate, they also made it public. In moving the experience of the Second Birth from the private to the public sphere, the revivalists simultaneously expanded and diminished the religious role of women. On the one hand revivalism gave middle-class women opportunities to break out of the woman's sphere. Women were central to evangelism, with one observer noting that "in all instances, where they were most active, revivals were most powerful." Traditionally women were active in prayer meetings that preceded revivals. During the 1820s this role increased as men and women joined together to pray in "small circles" for the conversion of individuals, first in Finney's revivals and then throughout the North. Women were also formidable fundraisers and organizers for formalist revivals. On the other hand the rise of professional evangelists, who among formal evangelicals were always men, removed the act of conversion from divine to male hands. Male authority was further enhanced by formalist desires to keep women out of the public sphere. As the revivals progressed it became increasingly clear that while women sowed the seeds of salvation, men reaped the harvest.

Finney's greatest success was among the well-to-do, because his message and his methods paralleled those of the emerging commercial economy. From the moment they laid eyes on him, professionals, merchants, and prosperous artisans rightly suspected that Finney was a man who spoke their language. Unlike most formalist clergy, he forsook the usual elaborate clerical garb for "an unclerical suit of gray." In short, Finney looked like a businessman, and his listeners soon realized that he couched his theology in the language of the commercial center.

Four middle-class values—self-discipline, self-determination, systemization, and order—were prominent in the evangelist's message and ministry. Finney's promotion of self-discipline was particularly evident after 1830 when he toned down the emotional excesses of his early meetings and emphasized order and decorum in the sanctuary even during the emotional intensity of a revival. In the Rochester crusade of 1830–1831, Finney paired personal conversion with temperance, making the abstention from intoxicating drink proof that an individual's experience with God was genuine. Self-determination was prominent as Finney argued that salvation was available not just to a preordained elect but to whomever would choose to join the Lord's army. Finney's love of systemization became clear in 1835 when he published his *Lectures on Revivals of Religion*. Finney argued that a revival was "not a miracle or dependent on a miracle in any sense" but was rather based on scientific laws as was physics or engineering. All any evangelist, or revival engineer, had to do was to employ Finney's scientific means and he would convert dozens, if not hundreds, of souls. While Finney borrowed many of the techniques of such antiformalists as the Methodists, his love of order kept them from offending middle-class sensibilities. The evangelist would not permit the "loud praying and pounding on benches" that accompanied antiformalist religious rallies, noting that "inquirers needed more opportunity to think than they had when there was so much noise."

Despite the success of Taylor, Beecher, and Finney's New School innovations, traditionalists retained enormous power in formalist circles. Taylor managed to escape censure, but Beecher was tried for heresy by the Presbytery of Cincinnati in 1835. Finney found the confines of Presbyterianism too constricting, left the denomination, and became an independent Congregationalist in the mid-1830s. But the New School movement had grown too large to be stopped by removing its leaders. In 1837 the traditionalist majority expelled the New School faction (almost half of total membership) from the Presbyterian church. The New School faction promptly organized its own General Assembly and competed against the Old School until after the Civil War.

Even as Finney was reaching the peak of his influence, a new form of formalist religion—devotionalism—gained power after 1830. Devotionalism was particularly attractive to urban middle-class women because it gave them a social role that was in theory equal to, but not equivalent to, that of their husbands. With their husbands "winning the bread" away from the house, women assumed nearly exclusive responsibility for raising the children. Not only were women supposed to teach their offspring the values of hard work, honesty, thrift, and obedience, all of which would ensure future success in the business world, but they were to bring their children to saving faith. This latter role received national validation in 1847 when Horace Bushnell published *Christian Nurture*. Bushnell rejected the revivalist ethos outright, arguing that a life-changing conversion experience was unnecessary. Instead of waiting for children to receive Christ during an adolescent crisis, Bushnell maintained "that the child is to grow up a Christian, and never know himself as being otherwise." With this statement Bushnell removed the mantle of evangelistic responsibility from the professional revivalist and placed it on the shoulders of the Victorian mother.

By the 1850s devotionalism had made significant inroads into areas once dominated by traditionalists and New School theologians. Religion no longer focused on God the Father, a deity who may or may not have given people free will regarding salvation, but rather on a loving Jesus who exhibited the feminine virtues of obedience, submission, gentleness, and long-suffering faithfulness. Instead of emphasizing correct doctrine or saving grace, devotionalists sought a closer walk with Jesus, a Savior who not only atoned for the sins of all but who befriended and solved the personal problems of those who loved him. With the success of devotionalism, formal evangelicalism was barely distinguishable from nonevangelical forms of Christianity. Devotionalists believed that a personal commitment to Christ was necessary for salvation, but they also maintained that conversion need not be internally disruptive in any way. Instead children could grow in their knowledge of God and commit themselves to Jesus at a very early age.

While the conversions of formal evangelicals were relatively orderly, antiformalists understood the Second Birth to be both democratic and emotional. The religious populism characteristic of Methodists and Baptists extended to conversion, as these two groups headed for the frontier and brought tens of thousands of ordinary folk into their folds. Religious fervor, cried the populists, was the only thing God respected. Formalist wealth, prestige, and education meant nothing to the Almighty—only a life dedicated to Him mattered. Antiformalists believed that the emotions could not stand idle while people passed from death unto life; they expected conversions to be emotional and were suspicious of claimed transformations that did not have the requisite drama.

The most prominent antiformal group, the Methodists, preached a democratic theory of conversion known as Arminianism. This doctrine maintained that God did not choose who would be saved or damned; that Christ died for all sinners, not just an elect few; and that individuals could determine their own eternal fate by accepting Jesus or continuing to follow the devil. Evangelical Arminianism in the United States appealed most to social outsiders who believed that elites used Calvinism as a way to monopolize religion. Antiformalists identified Calvinism as the faith of the comfortable and privileged few while less prestigious groups did the true work of God. Peter Cartwright, the Methodist circuit rider, boasted how "the illiterate Methodist preachers actually set the world on fire, (the American world at least,) while [the Calvinists] were lighting their matches!"

Antiformalists were not surprised that Calvinists promoted predestination, as they suspected the Calvinists assumed that they, not the poor, were God's chosen few. Methodists attacked the Calvinist theory of election as not only undemocratic (by negating the human will and restricting salvation to a few) but as unscriptural and a violation of common sense. Perhaps the greatest criticism that Methodists leveled against predestination was that it kept people from seeking salvation. When James Finley was a young man his father asked him why he did not pray. The young Finley responded, "Because I do not see any use in it. If I am one of the elect, I will be saved in God's good time; and if I am one of the non-elect, praying will do me no good, as Christ did not die for them."

Officially Baptists were Calvinists, but for the most part they operated as Arminians when it came to saving souls. One Baptist missionary noted the similarity between Western Baptist and Methodist preaching in that both were "very controversial and most bitter against Calvinists." Baptists were able to slip away from their Calvinist origins because they placed ultimate ecclesiastical authority in the hands of the local congregation. Recognizing no authority but the Bible, local congregations avoided the conundrums of Calvinism by downplaying doctrine, emphasizing the human role in conversion, and trying to convert as many sinners as the Methodists.

Unlike the formalists, Methodists and Baptists did not try to "restrain the Spirit." Powerful emotions were proof of conversion, not a hindrance to understanding doctrine. Anti-formalists wanted spontaneous worship that was free to move whichever way God might lead. The camp meeting embraced both democracy and emotionalism and dominated antiformal evangelism in the early nineteenth century. While Presbyterians created the essential elements of the camp meeting in their eighteenth-century sacramental meetings, the camp meeting did not become a staple of nineteenth-century life until it was adopted by the Methodists. The white population was widely dispersed in the new states of Kentucky and Tennessee. Usually Methodists dealt with this problem by having their ministers "ride the circuit" by periodically visiting homes and class meetings. The problem with this approach was that it could take a circuit rider six weeks to make one trip around the five-hundred-mile circuit, making it impossible for the minister to preach regularly to any group of people. In 1800 a group of Methodist, Baptist, and Presbyterian ministers decided to preach to thousands of people for an extended period of time. Instead of sending the minister to the people, they had the people come to the minister. The eighteen clerics planned a four-day meeting, sent fliers across two states, and cleared a site near Gasper River, Kentucky, so that people coming from forty to a hundred miles away could camp out in tents overnight between the day-long preaching services. The meeting was successful in the eyes of its promoters, and additional meetings were held in the summer and fall of 1800.

The Cane Ridge revival in 1801 further popularized the camp meeting as an antiformal evangelistic tool. The Cane Ridge meeting was spectacular both in terms of its size and its activities. Observers estimated that between 10,000 and 25,000 people attended. At any given moment as many as seven preachers—speaking separately—each had huge crowds hanging on their every word. The masses that attended Cane Ridge were both emotional and vocal; the audience laughed, cried, shouted, and sang in response to the minister's message. One participant described the resulting noise to be "like the roar of Niagara." Cane Ridge was so noted for its physical expressions of religiosity that cynics referred to the events there as "acrobatic Christianity." Saints, seekers, and sinners frequently experienced what one observer called "the jerks," in which "hundreds of men and women would commence jerking backward and forward with great rapidity and violence, so much so that their bodies would bend so as to bring their heads near to the floor, and the hair of the women would crack like the lash of the driver's whip." When a preacher was driving home the horror of hell and the glories of heaven, many in his audience sometimes stiffened, toppled over, and laid in a semiconscious state from a few minutes to twenty-four hours. "At one time," a witness related, "I saw at least five hundred swept down in a moment, as if a battery of a thousand guns had been opened upon them, and then immediately followed shrieks and shouts that rent the very heavens. My hair rose up on my head, my whole frame trembled, the blood ran cold in my veins..."

By 1820 the camp meeting was the central feature of Methodist evangelism. In that year alone almost one thousand encampments were held across the United States. No longer restricted to the frontier, camp meetings were held on the east coast near urban areas. As camp meetings grew in popularity, they lost some of the bizarre behavior that characterized Cane Ridge. Jerking and falling largely disappeared as the newly redeemed now expressed their joy through the more understandable means of leaping and shouting. In its mature phase the camp meeting had a predictable format whereby the five-step process of conversion, an event that could take months or years according to traditional Calvinists, was often compressed into a four-day period. In the ideal case, seekers, scoffers, and the merely curious would be convicted, experience great emotional discomfort, receive an emotional release upon conversion, testify to saving grace, and finally integrate their lives with fellow believers by joining a church and participating in Communion by meeting's end.

During the encampment clergy and laity each played specific roles in encouraging conversions. The first stage, conviction, was the responsibility of the preacher. Religious services were held throughout the day, with ministers taking turns on the elevated platform. Preachers began by quoting a specific scriptural text but used it as a launching pad rather than as an organizing device. Once into the sermon, ministers emphasized the sinfulness of mankind, the horrors of hell, the glories of heaven, and the necessity of seeking God immediately. Homey examples and folk illustrations elaborated each point. Should anyone doubt their sinfulness, preachers attacked a wide variety of frontier vices. Should all else fail, there was always the Methodist "trinity of devils to fight, namely superfluous dress, whisky, and slavery." The goal of each sermon was to "strike fire" or bring a powerful emotional response from the preacher's listeners.

Once the preacher had struck fire and many appeared to be under conviction, he stepped down from the platform and joined a host of believers who had sprung into action to exhort the awakened. At this point struggling sinners exhibited great emotion as they wrestled with a sense of guilt. Crying, wailing, and other signs of emotional distress appeared as the convicted struggled to separate themselves from their past "sinful" lives. The symbolic step of separation was to leave their place in the crowd and move forward to seats (called mourners' benches) directly in front of the speaker's stand. The decision to go forward was difficult because conversion meant rejecting secular life, abandoning old pleasures, and joining a church that had extremely strict behavioral codes. Realizing that those in distress needed encouragement, numerous lay people (including women and children) and clergy served as exhorters who milled around the audience and pleaded with the convicted to step forward. One by one, mourners experienced emotional release, assurance of God's acceptance, and a belief they had attained eternal life.

Both the convert and the church community recognized the individual's new status after the experience of grace. New believers went to instructional sessions where they were told what was expected of those who professed saving faith. Converts also attended the love feast, a communal gathering usually held toward the end of the camp meeting, where they shared bread and water and told everyone what they had experienced. In Baptist camp meetings the newly redeemed were led down to a nearby river where they were baptized by immersion and were granted church membership. Methodists usually had acceptance ceremonies toward the end of their encampments as well. New confessors were welcomed into a local class (a fellowship group of approximately fifteen people), were placed on probation (usually for six months), and were admitted as full members if they lived a strict, moral life during the probationary period. Camp meetings ended with "closing exercises" where converts joined other believers in a march around the campsite, once again demonstrating the new believer's status within the community of saints.

Camp meetings were not only religious meetings, they were social gatherings for the whole community. Geographically, saints and seekers occupied the worship and encampment areas in the center of the meeting area. Socializers and scoffers pitched their tents in an outer ring where they could pursue their own activities without being disturbed by enthusiastic preachers and their emotionally wrought audiences. While those in the center focused on religious conversion, the out-dwellers were most interested in selling and consuming whiskey, gambling, fornicating, and brawling. Frequently the two groups came into conflict. On more than one occasion Peter Cartwright left the preacher's stand to battle rowdies intent on breaking up his meeting. Prosperous women often saw the camp meeting as an opportunity to find prospective mates and to show off their finery, while prostitutes saw the encampment, with its many thousands of men in a relatively confined area, as an unusual opportunity to make money. Emotional religion and sexual license both flourished in the camp environment. Many encampments set up patrols which monitored the borders between the religious and the irreligious, but problems of violence and illicit sex were never fully eradicated.

Protracted meetings were a variation of camp meetings, and they eventually replaced the encampments as an evangelistic tool. Baptists preferred protracted meetings from the early nineteenth century, and Methodists (and New School Calvinists) came to prefer them as well. Protracted meetings were held inside a church building and continued every evening for several weeks. They were particularly useful in regions that had left the frontier stage of development and were part of a commercial network. Everyday economic activities were not interrupted as participants could perform their normal business functions by day and attend services at

night. In addition, the protracted meetings were much easier
to police as the walls of the church building were a natural
barrier between religionists and town rowdies.

Despite the importance of camp and protracted meetings,
many antiformalist conversions occurred away from mass
gatherings. One such instance occurred in central New York,
after George Peck, a local circuit rider, visited James Andrews, a young, recently married farmer. Peck counseled
Andrews regarding his soul, then left the field where they
spoke and returned to the farmhouse. Moments later Andrews's mother found the young farmer lying in a field,
and she shouted, "O dear me, the horse has kicked James!"
After Peck rushed back to the field he found Andrews and
his parents "with their arms around each other, reeling this
way and that, James shouting, 'Glory to God!' and all three
weeping, praising the Lord, and acting as if they were wild
with joy."

By the 1840s and 1850s antiformalist religion was less
emotional and conversions occurred less frequently than in
earlier years. A major factor in this change was that Methodists and Baptists prospered, gained influence and status,
and moved toward the political and economic center of
American society. They also adopted some of the formalist
religious patterns that characterized evangelical Episcopalians, Presbyterians, and Congregationalists. The tendency to
formalize was strongest in the urban North. Well-to-do New
York City Methodists found an important ally in Nathan
Bangs, a prominent minister who stressed orderly worship
and believed that "clapping of the hands, screaming, and
even jumping...marred and disgraced the work of God."

Generational change was another factor that undercut
emotional religion during the 1840s and 1850s. This decline
occurred partly because the religion's adherents generally

grew up in the faith rather than having consciously chosen it, and tended to take their religion for granted. Although camp meetings continued after 1820, more and more Methodists and Baptists grew up in the faith than were converted to it. As a result they were also less enthusiastic about their Christianity and found it difficult to experience dramatic conversions that sharply differentiated between their life in "the world" and their life after redemption.

But Methodists did not simply mimic the formalists and move toward the relatively tranquil childhood conversions of maternal Christian Nurture. Instead some Methodists maintained emotional religion by transferring the climactic event in a Christian's life from conversion to "the second blessing," an event in which the Holy Spirit brought the Christian purity of heart. Phoebe Palmer, the principal figure in the holiness movement that promoted the second blessing, grew up in the home of devout New York City Methodists. Palmer experienced giving her heart to Jesus at such an early age that she could not point to the moment of her conversion. Throughout her twenties and thirties Palmer wondered if she was a true Christian because she did not have the dramatic conversion experience considered necessary for salvation. In the course of her struggle Palmer accepted John Wesley's doctrine of entire sanctification, also known as evangelical perfection or the second blessing, which stated that personal holiness came as a gift from God, that Christians could overcome the "inbred sin" that remained in their lives even after conversion, and that total submission to Jesus would result in sinless perfection. Individuals who were sanctified, according to Palmer, received the witness of the Holy Spirit in the emotions, thus producing an experience in many ways similar to conversion. Palmer's experience of entire sanctification in 1837 finally gave her the emotional proof she needed to be convinced she was truly a Christian. In 1843 she published *The Way of Holiness* which spread her teachings among second- and third-generation urban Methodists whose conversions came too early to remember but whose tradition demanded that God touch their hearts in a remarkable manner.

Black Americans experienced the most tumultuous conversions among antebellum evangelicals. Being "struck dead" by the power of God was the norm for African American conversions long after the Civil War. Even more than white antiformalists, blacks believed such otherworldly experiences as dreams and visions to be an integral part of the Christian life.

In order to understand African American conversion experiences, it is necessary to look at West African religion, which was a rich source of slave culture. In African religions, humans lived in the physical world but had to deal successfully with two kinds of spiritual beings immediately above them if they were to prosper. The living dead (those who had died relatively recently and who were still remembered by name) were directly above humans. Like kinfolk within a specific community, they were closely tied to their descendants. Africans were expected to venerate the living dead; the departed would reciprocate by rewarding faithful descendants with longevity and prosperity, and by punishing the neglectful with disease or other personal disasters. The divinities (mythic leaders, founders of clans, and the spirits of ordinary folk who died in the distant past) often had greater powers than the living dead and could direct natural elements such as weather and animals, as well as intervene directly in the lives of human beings. Both the living dead and the divinities were unpredictable and dangerous, and priests and mediums were needed to discern their wishes and appease them. The High God, by far the most powerful figure in the sacred cosmos, operated far above humans, the living dead, and the divinities. The High God created the world, combated evil and worked for good, and presided over all other beings, but did not actively influence the affairs of humankind.

Africans believed that spirits (the divinities and living dead) communicated their desires to humans through sacred ceremonies. Typically tribesfolk danced in a circle using the whole body, including hands, feet, belly, and hips. The circle moved counterclockwise and was driven by beating drums which set the pace of the dance and called up the spirits. The community supported the dancers by encouraging them through hand-clapping, foot-tapping, and antiphonal (call-and-response) exhortation and singing. The song and dance were continuously repeated, steadily increasing in speed and intensity, until the emotions of the dancers and their observers were at fever pitch. At this point the dancers had fully opened themselves to the spirits, and the lesser gods and/or divinities responded by "mounting" the participants and dancing them in front of the community. The spirit had now totally absorbed the individual personalities of the dancers, and each possessed person, in a trance, paraded in the spirit's emblems and colors, and sampled the spirit's favorite foods.

Once slaves were Christianized, many African religious practices were given a new meaning. Rhythmic singing, preaching, and shouting were continued but in praise of a Christian God. Blacks still sought ecstatic experience, but the experience of the Holy Spirit was qualitatively different from possession by a tribal spirit. In the Christian context the enraptured believer's personality was not replaced by another being. Rather, the Holy Spirit filled the believer with happiness and power, and the believer had no choice but to sing, shout, and dance in response to the spirit's acting on his or her soul. The "ring shout" or "running spirituals" were central to slave worship, and black evangelicals used the "ring shout" to call on the Holy Spirit. The shout was so central to slave worship that when white missionaries and free urban blacks (whose religion was more acculturated) tried to suppress it, slaves invariably resisted, protesting that "without a ring sinners won't get converted."

Unlike white evangelicals, African American evangelicals were not obsessed with doctrinal quarrels over the nature of conversion. Predestination had little appeal to slaves, as it implied that God intended their involuntary servitude. Concern for theological abstractions paled beside the more practical question of how to obtain eternal life. While African American evangelicals agreed that having a conversion experience was essential to gaining salvation, what they thought important was the fact of conversion, not theories about how the process of conversion occurred.

Interviews in the late 1920s show that African American slaves typically fell into a deep trance where they visited the eternal realms of heaven and hell. By contrast, European American dreams and visions were usually limited to a single phenomenon such as a visit by a warm and compassionate Jesus or the presence of a light that caused all objects within a room to glow. Whites, unlike blacks, were not transported to a different reality but saw only an alteration of ordinary experience.

Black conversions occurred in a variety of places and circumstances, in groups and in private. Many blacks were already under conviction and sought release in church. Many others experienced grace at camp meetings (which usually were segregated until the last day), at revival meetings, or at the hush harbors. Slave worship reinforced community solidarity and the communal rite of conversion; still, many slaves experienced conversion alone as they underwent a period of "striving." The African precedent for this approach was the initiation ceremony into the cult of the gods, when individuals went into the bush first for a period of self-purification. Baptists in the Sea Islands of South Carolina encouraged those under conviction to undergo a long process of prayer and self-examination "in the bush" as they sought personal conversion.

Many African Americans who had no conscious desire to get right with God experienced sudden conversion while working in the cotton fields, chopping wood in a forest, piling lumber, or playing "in a crap game out on the Harding pike." Those who experienced unexpected conversion often expressed amazement that they were among the chosen: "I don't know why it was I got converted because I had been doing nearly everything they told me I ought not to do."

Whether conversion was sought or totally unexpected, narratives inevitably began with a voice speaking to the future convert. Sometimes the voice was inward; other times it came from the environment and the hearer looked for a human source. A slave named Morte said he "jumped because I thought it was my master coming to scold and whip me for plowing up some more corn." Sometimes the voice brought a comforting message, but more often it conveyed the warning, "You got to die and can't live."

Shortly after hearing the voice, the convert was immobilized and entered a trance often described as a form of death. One convert recalled, "I was in my house alone and I declare unto you when His power struck me I died. I fell out on the floor flat on my back. I could neither speak nor move for my tongue stuck to the roof of my mouth; my jaws were locked and my limbs were stiff." Others claimed to have become "weak and faint" or "just heavy" immediately before having a divine vision.

Once in the conversion trance, individuals usually traveled to hell where they saw the horrors of damnation and struggled over the state of their souls. The portrayal of hell was graphic. One convert insisted he "saw old Satan chained about his chest and legs in a square pit. He just stood staring at me and moving his club-foot." Another saw "a deep chasm filled with ravenous beasts and old satan was there with a ball and chain on his leg. He had a great ball in his hand and threw this at me but it missed." To compound the horror, those in the trance frequently saw those they had known in life who were "were just roaming and staggering along" and "saying, 'Oh, how long?'" The horror reached a climax when travelers saw their own condition. Frequently they saw themselves dangling over the flames of hell or split in two, with a smaller self looking over the old dead self that was perched "on the very brinks of hell." This idea of two selves appears to have been carried over from West Africa, as many tribes believed in an inner self or soul that was distinct and could be removed from the outer self or the body.

At this point the convert invariably cried out for God's mercy. In every case the Lord responded quickly by providing a visible means of escape, demonstrating to the traveler that his or her soul had been spared and salvation had been accomplished. Sometimes hell's visitors escaped by using God-given angel wings, a heavenly chariot, a divine ladder, or by following a comforting voice. Most often help came in the form of "a little man, very small and with waxen hair." Invariably the little man (who was usually white) gave words of comfort, urged the convert to follow him, and led the way eastward to the gates of heaven. Paradise was described in a number of ways but most often as a huge beautiful city, as a huge room where all God's children sat eating around a table, or as "a beautiful green pasture [where] there were thousands of sheep and they turned towards me and all in one bleat cried out, 'Welcome! Welcome! to the House of God.'" In most accounts God was a dominating personal force who had at last set things in proper order and rewarded the righteous with everlasting life.

Individual slaves experienced in different ways the final two stages of the conversion process. Sometimes recognition and reintegration occurred while the convert was still in the trance. After one man was lifted over the gulf of hell, he reported, "I looked at my hands and they looked new. I looked at my feet and they looked new too." He went on to experience divine acceptance, as "there was the heavenly host of angels and they all said, Welcome! Welcome!" At other times the last two stages of conversion occurred directly after the trance. One woman professed that "When I came to I looked at myself and I was all new.... I began shouting and praising God." An ex-slave named Mary reported that within a week after she regained consciousness, she "went to church ... having been directed in the spirit to an old preacher named Rev. Mason who, after hearing my testimony, reached me among his flock."

The conversion trance allowed slaves to go through the redemptive process in a specifically African manner. While traditional Calvinists saw conversion as taking months or years, and Methodists compressed the period of conversion into the camp meeting's four days, African Americans had trances that moved them through all five stages in a matter of hours. The rapidity of the process appears to be linked to the perceived closeness of God. Groups that believed God to be very near, rather than simply transcendent, tended to have dramatic, quick conversions, and Americans who drew inspiration from their African heritage, which drew no sharp distinction between the secular and the sacred, had the most stunning, rapid transformations of all. Just as African worship went beyond "head" and "heart" to involve the body, African American conversion was not just an intellectual or an emotional event but a totally soul-stunning experience, physically felt.

For many slaves the conversion trance was only the first step in the world of the supernatural. Many reported having dreams, visions, and premonitions for years afterward. Believers reporting these phenomena maintained that these experiences were part of the way their Heavenly Father spoke to his children. Most ongoing accounts tell of angels, heavenly ladders, or celestial objects appearing to give the faithful direction or confidence. A few believed God revealed the future through such experiences. One woman claimed she saw Jesus in a vision and "this time it was a warning of death. I saw in the west one evening, a cloud and in it I first saw a man's foot but as I looked I saw the head exposed at another point in the cloud.... About a month after this a very dear uncle of mine died and I think that this vision was a warning." In Africa the power to see the future belonged to the priest-king; among black Southern evangelicals such powers were claimed by those whom God especially touched.

The stunning nature of slave conversion narratives suggests that conversion played a different emotional role for black slaves than it did for whites. Formalists and antiformalists looked to conversion as proof of their salvation; African Americans saw conversion as proof that God recognized them in a society that gave them so little recognition. One ex-slave testified that as a result of her dramatic conversion, "I say that a child that has been truly born of God knows it...the law is written in my heart and I don't need no book." Another regarded his conversion as God's "spiritual answer of approval" that gave him confidence. Shortly before he attempted his escape from slavery, he heard "a voice like thunder" that told him "though wicked men hunt you, trust in me, for I am the Rock of your Defense."

While this portrayal of religious conversion fits most antebellum black evangelicals, some blacks experienced conversion and worshiped God in ways that deviated from the African American norm. Just as white antiformalists lost some of their exuberance when they rose in social status, some black evangelicals downplayed African aspects of worship when they moved beyond the status of bondsmen. The tendency toward acculturation was strongest in the North where blacks were heavily outnumbered by whites and where African Americans had some chance at vocational and educational advancement. Thus some Northern free blacks experienced conversion and preferred worship styles that were less overtly African than those in the South. But the dominant influence in shaping antebellum black religion was the overwhelming power of the Southern, African-oriented majority.

The impact of emotional, revivalist religion was felt far beyond the evangelical community. Christians from other traditions began to mirror evangelicalism and to stress conversion experiences. By mid-century, when a number of evangelicals deemphasized revivalism in favor of feminine, devotional, and domestic religion, American culture was moving in a parallel, feminized direction.

Although American revivalism was an evangelical inven-

tion, it spread beyond evangelical circles between 1820 and
1860. Its use can be seen in three traditionally nonevangelical
groups—the Quakers, Lutherans, and Roman Catholics.

By the 1820s evangelical ideas had become controversial
among Quakers. While country Friends were more successful in continuing the traditional Quaker life-style which
emphasized plain speech, dress, and homes, city Friends
reflected the larger commercial culture, wearing "plain"
clothes made of the finest fabric and living in well-furn-
ished, luxurious houses. In addition, country Friends maintained the traditional emphasis on the "inner light" while
city Friends often adopted the evangelical themes of *Sola
Scriptura*, social reform, and the need for a saving, inner
experience of grace. The "evangelicalization" of Quakerism
alienated traditionalists, and the two groups battled for
control of the movement. In 1827 the Friends split perma-
nently into two, both sides claiming to be the true heirs of
the Quaker tradition. Some Friends gravitated toward Elias
Hicks, who denied that the Bible had any unique authority,
rejected original sin, and saw Jesus as being unimportant,
except as an example of one who was "wholly given over to
following the Inner Light." The "evangelical" Friends called
the Hicksites heretics (even though Hicksite teaching was
closer to traditional Quakerism than was their own), renamed themselves the Orthodox Friends, and in essence
became another evangelical denomination.

In central Pennsylvania a similar controversy emerged
among German-speaking Lutherans. Traditionally Lutherans were critical of American revivalists, particularly the
Methodists, calling them "fanatics," "head-hangers," "knee-
sliders," and "foot-stampers." But as later generations of
Lutherans came to have greater contact with American
culture, their English-speaking leaders began to advocate

revivalist methods. Among Lutherans the leading "evangelical" figure was Samuel Schmucker, founder of Gettys-
burg Seminary. Schmucker's followers, known as "American
Lutherans" or "New Measure Lutherans," often held protracted meetings which they renamed "special conferences"
to pacify their more traditionalist brethren. The special
conferences included altar-calls, exhorting, shouting, and
Lutherans "falling as dead" when convicted of sin.

Nor did American Catholics escape revivalist practices.
Although the "parish mission" was imported from Europe,
by the 1850s it was remarkably similar to evangelical revivalism. The goal of the mission was to reclaim sinners and
encourage the faithful. One mission manual, a Catholic
equivalent to Finney's *Lectures on Revivals of Religion*, declared that "a true mission is that which, after restoring the
grace of God to those who have fallen, renews the people in
their belief in Christ and the Church, teaches sound principles of morality, and reestablishes the pious frequentation of
the Sacraments." In order to restore faith among lukewarm
Catholics, the parish mission employed many tactics similar
to those of the Protestants. Missions lasted from eight days to
two weeks, with brief services in the morning, teaching
sessions during the day, and the main attraction at night. At
the evening service, a priest-evangelist, usually a specially
trained Redemptorist or Jesuit, began worship with music,
song, and prayers, and then delivered an hour-long sermon.
At the end of the mission the preacher held up a white
baptismal robe to remind people of their baptismal vows.
According to one priest, this tactic "set the people almost
frantic; all the preacher said after this was drowned in the
uproar." Catholics streamed forward to confess their sins,
lining up to enter a vast array of confessionals set up for the
occasion. When the evening's work was done the priest-

evangelist, like the circuit rider who counted converts, measured his success by the number of confessions and communions that had taken place that night.

By the time American Catholics implemented the parish mission, enthusiastic revivalism was beginning to wane and devotionalism was growing in many evangelical circles. With men absent because of business, women became the spiritual directors of their households, and they preferred intense, private, and personal devotion to rambunctious and tumultuous conversions. The assumption was that if housewives performed their spiritual duties properly, their children would grow gradually in the faith and would never need to undergo the "trauma" of conversion. Part of this strategy was to emphasize Jesus, the children's friend, the ever faithful confidant, the sacrificial victim, the female alter ego, rather than the more powerful and demanding figure of God the Father. By getting their children to bond to Jesus, evangelical females also tied their offspring closer to themselves. The end result of the domestication of religion was a feminized and sentimentalized faith.

The feminization of evangelicalism was part of a broader feminization of American culture. As urban men became more and more concerned with commercial activity, middle- and upper-class women became the stewards of the culture. Book venders catered to female desires, and as a result published literature changed. The essay continued to be a popular literary form, but fiction and poetry, especially the romantic and sentimental variety, absorbed a growing share of the book market. Sir Walter Scott and Charles Dickens undercut critics' attacks on the novel by writing works that even Lyman Beecher could appreciate. Most novels, however, were not written by British men but by, to use Hawthorne's caustic words, "a damned mob of scribbling women." Female authors produced scores of moralistic and sentimental novels which portrayed life in domestic settings. Together these novels emphasized the joys of self-sacrifice, the nobility of suffering, the correctness of conventional morality, and the need for women to be connected to family, home, and church. Besides providing an imaginary "sisterhood" with whom readers could identify and storylines with an underlying eroticism, the novels gave women suggestions on how to handle difficulties in their daily lives. Should fiction fail to provide guidelines for handling life's problems, a great many ladies' magazines and self-improvement books were available to answer remaining questions. By mid-century religion and culture were so domesticated that religious eclectic and writer Orestes Brownson grumbled, "The curse of our age is its feminity [and] its lack, not of barbarism, but of virility."

3

A Just and Holy Life

EVEN THOUGH urban formalists gravitated toward Christian Nurture by mid-century, the vast majority of evangelicals still believed that religious conversion was essential to the Christian life. They also agreed that the Second Birth was only the first step in the journey of faith. Once saved, each believer was expected to live a just and holy life.

Although they did not believe that good works brought them salvation, antebellum evangelicals had many reasons for emphasizing proper behavior. The first was obedience to God. If one called oneself a Christian, and experienced God's grace through conversion, how could one not help but follow God's dictates? As Jesus said, "If ye love me, keep my commandments." Second, evangelicals lived an upright life to demonstrate the validity of their conversion experiences. Jesus pointed out that "every good tree bringeth forth good fruit; but a corrupt tree bringeth forth evil fruit." So it is with human beings: "by their fruits ye shall know them." Third, evangelicals emphasized godly behavior in order to "witness" to the world. Jesus said, "By this shall all men know that ye are my disciples, if ye have love one to another." The goal was to be so loving, so good, so pure, that unregenerate sinners would be convicted of their own sin and seek salvation. Fourth, evangelicals "hungered after righteousness" as a form of self-discipline in order to keep their thoughts on heavenly glories rather than be distracted by earthly temptations. Jesus warned that "No man can serve two masters." One must choose between God and mammon. Fifth, by becoming a just and holy people, evangelicals believed they were bringing the Kingdom of God to earth, fulfilling the phrase in the Lord's Prayer, "Thy will be done in earth, as it is in Heaven." Granted, many evangelicals viewed the Kingdom to be no larger than their local congregation. But if the believers were faithful, sinners would be convicted and the borders of the Kingdom would grow. Perhaps in time the entire nation could be converted to the ways of righteousness.

All five rationales for doing good promoted personal discipline and self-control. When faced with temptation, believers were expected to defer (or deny) immediate gratification and protect their Christian reputation so that at some future point they could convert others to Jesus. In a sense, evangelicals exhibited a spiritual form of republican virtue in that they were willing to set aside personal interests to promote the common good of the Kingdom of God.

Maintaining religious values in a secular culture would have been difficult for individuals operating alone. But antebellum evangelicals had two systems that helped them perpetuate their ethos. The traditional system employed the support and reinforcement received from the local church. The second, or more modern approach, utilized the individualistic doctrine of perfectionism which contended that personal sanctification came directly from the Holy Spirit.

To some degree all evangelicals were traditionalists in that they placed great value on the local congregation as a community of believers who shared a common conversion experience and thus a common identity as the people of

God. The local congregation was an institution where believers could get support for daily struggles against secular society and where they could release pent-up emotions. Formalists expressed themselves at prayer meetings. Baptist fellowships regularly held covenant meetings where they inquired about the "state of feeling" of the gathered brothers and sisters. Methodists refused to allow non-Methodists to attend class meetings and love feasts because the inclusion of "unawakened" persons inhibited the "liberty of speech" that bound believers together. African Americans expressed themselves most fully in their hush harbors. In each of these situations evangelical leaders inquired into the state of member souls, and believers used the opportunity to speak to the joys and frustrations of trying to live an evangelical life in a nonevangelical world.

If traditionalists saw each congregation as the local manifestation of the Kingdom of God, they viewed the larger secular community as part of Satan's Kingdom, which they usually referred to as "the world." This other kingdom was part of an evil triumvirate, "the world, the flesh, and the devil," which sought to destroy the faith of believers. Evangelical churches frequently quoted portions of Scripture that advised distance from worldly things. In 1837 the Baptist journal *Religious Herald* explained, "A public profession of Christianity is an avowal of our separation from the world, as regards its maxims, pursuits, and pleasures.... We view ourselves as strangers and pilgrims on earth, looking for a better, even a heavenly country." Because they were "born again," evangelicals abstained from "fleshly lusts" and "idle amusements" to commit themselves to a "love of holiness" and "communion with God."

Because it was so important to keep a distinct line separating the believers from the world, evangelical congregations used a system of church discipline to reinforce member self-discipline. Each fellowship monitored member behavior, not because of meddlesomeness but because believers needed the support of the faithful to vanquish the devil, the world, and the flesh. In addition, surveillance was necessary to protect the church. Sin was a disease that could infect the entire body. To protect itself and keep the disease from spreading, the church had to rid itself of the sin or, if need be, the sinner. When believers strayed from correct conduct, the local congregation worked to bring them back to accepted behavioral norms. The first step was to send a committee to counsel the offending individual. If the subject of the visit admitted his or her error and was willing to repent before the church, the matter was dropped. But if the visitation committee could not "gain satisfaction," the matter went before the congregation (or before the elder board—usually called "the session"—in the Presbyterian church) which placed the offender on trial. After hearing the evidence the congregation or session judged the defendant. If found guilty the parishioner would have to confess and repent of wrongdoing or face excommunication from the church. Even if the member was excluded from fellowship, evangelical concern regarding his or her welfare did not end. Church members worked informally for repentance; should excluded members admit wrong and ask forgiveness, the congregation restored them to full membership.

Evangelical denominations generally agreed on what activities were unacceptable. First there was consensus that those who failed to attend church or who neglected other basic duties such as family prayer had to repent or be punished. Those who skipped worship not only neglected their own souls but weakened the local congregation, the primary support system for everyone's faith. In some congregations parishioners had to stand up and publicly explain to the assembled sisters and brethren why they had missed church the previous Sunday.

Second, evangelicals, like all Christians, contended that believers should obey the Ten Commandments. Thus members who swore, lied, committed adultery, or physically harmed other people were brought before the church, tried, and, if found guilty, either repented or were expelled. These investigations generated little controversy as members agreed that these offenses were major infractions of divine law. Keeping the Sabbath, however, was a touchier subject. While most evangelicals considered Sunday to be the appointed day of rest, groups such as the Seventh-Day Baptists believed the Old Testament command had not changed and that God still viewed Saturday as the Sabbath. Even Sunday observers found it difficult to achieve consensus. Did honoring the Sabbath mean refraining from work (a limited interpretation) or avoiding *everything* that was not overtly religious (a broad interpretation)? Evangelical leaders tended to favor the broader definition. For example, a Northern Congregational church banned the following from Sunday activities: traveling, visiting, worldly conversation, reading newspapers and nonreligious books, taking an unnecessary walk, and doing anything regarding food or dress that could be done on Saturday or Monday. Disciples of Christ clergy shared the same sentiments, with founder Alexander Campbell noting that those who go to or from church and "converse on the affairs of state, the times, the crops, the business of the pleasures of time and sense, show that their conversation is not in heaven." Lay evangelicals, however, did not always adhere to the broad definition. Some denominations resolved the confusion with a compromise: the leaders verbally supported the broad definition but enforced only the limited definition upon which everyone agreed. For example, North Carolina's Cape Fear Baptist Association condemned Sabbath violations ranging from "unnecessary visiting" to "trifling sports"; but those actually tried invariably were involved in commercial activities such as fishing, going to market, or starting a business trip on Sunday.

Third, evangelicals believed that church members should refrain from what was stigmatized as worldly activity. Much attention was paid to modifying hypermasculine behavior. Gambling was condemned, whether cardplaying, horseracing, or cockfighting. Socializing with the ungodly, often referred to as carousing or tavern haunting, was likewise forbidden. Surprisingly, at least for those familiar with twentieth-century evangelical taboos, little was said regarding tobacco. When the issue did arise, the chief complaint concerned cleanliness, as male parishioners frequently spit tobacco juice on the ground or church floor during worship. Of all of the male manifestations of worldliness, drunkenness received the most condemnation. Not only did inebriation run counter to the evangelical value of self-control, it often led to other unsanctioned activities such as brawling and sexual misconduct. To make matters worse, drunkenness was a public sin that undercut congregational claims of godliness.

While men were more likely to drink, women often had the worldly habit of novel-reading. This private practice supposedly inflamed the passions of impressionable women who wove their own fantasies into the text provided by the author, thus corrupting the sanctity of the home. In 1844 a Disciple of Christ revealed widespread fears when he wrote to the *Millennial Harbinger,* condemning novel-reading as "a waste of time," an activity that "dissipates and weakens the mind," and a practice that "predisposes to extravagance, and induces to crime."

Dances were condemned since they combined the public socializing of the male-oriented tavern and the imaginative romanticism of private female novel-reading. Evangelical opposition to dancing and balls was widespread and cut across social divisions. Episcopal Bishop William Meade maintained that dancing was one of the most popular manifestations of worldliness. The session of the Columbia (South Carolina) Presbyterian Church described member attendance at a recent ball as a "new tide of evil influence settling in upon the church." Barton Stone, of the Disciples of Christ, contended that of "all the fashionable amusements of the world," dancing "stands preeminent to captivate the mind, and to destroy all serious and religious impressions on the heart."

In the 1830s the traditional approach to holiness was challenged by the concept of "sinless perfection," which shifted the primary responsibility for holiness from the congregation to the individual. Perfectionists maintained that Christians could receive a second blessing from the Holy Spirit which would instantaneously complete the process of sanctification. Once people had received the second blessing they were free from willful sin. "Entire sanctification" meant, of course, that the disciplinary role of the local church was diminished. The strength to live a just life came not from being supervised by one's fellow believers; instead the ability to be good came from the fullness of the indwelling Holy Ghost.

While this doctrine of entire sanctification originated with John Wesley and then remained relatively quiet for about seventy years, it made a spectacular comeback in the 1830s. Charles Finney, who borrowed much of his thinking from the Methodists, experienced a "second conversion" and sought to integrate perfectionist teaching into a New School Calvinist framework. At approximately the same time Methodists rediscovered Wesley's teachings on entire sanctification. The Methodist holiness movement hit full stride in the mid-1830s when Sarah Lankford's "Tuesday Meetings for the Promotion of Holiness" began to spread perfectionist teaching in Methodist circles throughout the Northeast. The critical moment for the Methodist holiness revival came in 1837 when Phoebe Palmer (Sarah Lankford's sister) experienced the second blessing. Palmer's reinterpretation of Wesley's teaching—known as the "altar theology"—stressed two sacrifices. Justification came from accepting Christ's sacrifice of himself to atone for humanity's sin. Sanctification, or holiness, came when humans cast their entire beings on the "Altar, Christ." When individuals placed themselves on this altar to be sacrificed in the service of God, the fire of God would descend and their souls would be transformed by the "hallowing, consuming touch" of the Almighty. Thus purified, those who had experienced the second blessing were freed from personal willfulness and the habit of sinning.

While formal perfectionists gravitated toward Finney and antiformal perfectionists favored Palmer, the idea of spiritual self-improvement struck a general chord with pre–Civil War evangelicals. Perfectionism sanctified public male activism and private female piety, thus promoting the new evangelical personality. This teaching also enhanced the authority of the individual (who had been purified by divine action) over traditional human authorities such as the local congregation. Not surprisingly, both perfectionist movements were strongest in the Northeast where the growth of commercial culture fostered individualism and encouraged challenges to the traditional disciplinary powers of the local church. Perhaps

the most notable result of perfectionist teaching is that some
evangelical women used it to throw off the shackles of male
authority and assert a new independent public womanhood.
By arguing that God had infused them with holiness,
evangelical women challenged the private sphere and em-
barked on lives of public usefulness.

Before the Civil War, formal, antiformal, and African American evangelicals all strove to live just and holy lives. But the
way evangelicals pursued holiness varied greatly by social
location. The three groups differed in their emphasis and
approach to discipline, their concern over sins of pride, their
openness to perfectionism, and the direction in which women proceeded once they were liberated from the private
sphere.

Formalists viewed church disciplinary proceedings as only
one of many means available to promote virtuous Christian
living. Rather than carefully examining members for the
misuse of alcohol, intemperance could be fought more effectively through voluntary societies or by law. Using moral
suasion to advocate proper behavior via public education or
Sunday School was more effective than punishing moral
misdemeanors through church trials. Formalists were
community-minded folk, and they realized church discipline
was a limited tool that would work only on the more
compliant members of the church. It could never be the
basis for social reform and would never be the foundation
for a Christian America.

Perhaps most important, the strength of American individualism reduced the church's ability to discipline its male
members. Formal evangelical congregations attracted the
most commercialized, inner-directed, and self-motivated individuals. Such people chafed under ecclesiastical rules,

particularly if they had been converted believing that "salvation is a free choice and your decision to be saved is between you and God." Once accepted as members, individualists resisted church dictates, particularly over business affairs. Their position was strengthened in the 1830s when Charles Finney and other Oberlin perfectionists argued that sanctification came not from following church rules but as a second blessing from God. If God can make a believer perfect, what right did an imperfect church have to tell sanctified people what to do? While only a minority of formalists followed Finney to his most radical conclusions, many men supported his championing of the individual conscience, which in turn undercut the traditional supervisory role of the church.

Because formal evangelicals saw discipline as only one means to personal holiness, they were far less likely to indict or excommunicate members than were their antiformal brethren. In Cortland County, New York, for example, Congregationalist churches tried one-sixth as many cases each year as did Baptist churches, and Presbyterian fellowships prosecuted members at one-fourth the Baptist rate.

Formalists were most comfortable with the dominant culture, which also contributed to low levels of discipline. Congregationalists, Presbyterians, and Episcopalians saw themselves as providing moral leadership, and their members were found among the governing elite. Thus they were not psychologically driven to police carefully the borders dividing the church and "the world."

The formalist lack of concern over discipline helped promote internal harmony, but in the long term this reduced vigilance allowed secular values to enter the church. By the 1850s wealthy parishioners in New York circumscribed congregational abilities to regulate member business behavior. In the same decade Southern Presbyterian minister James

Henley Thornwell bemoaned worldliness within the church. "Fine houses, splendid organs, fashionable congregations— these seem to be the rage," he warned. "It is not asked, *what* a man preaches; but *where* he preaches, and to *whom*. If he has an imposing building, adorned with sofas for the rich to lounge on, where they are lulled into repose by an equally imposing orchestra, that is the place for a gentleman; and to go there twice on Sunday, is to worship God."

Formalist women faced an especially difficult situation because their ability to live active godly lives was impeded by formalist gender roles. While elite men found female piety commendable when it was restricted to the home and the church, they objected when women sought to use their talents publicly.

From the beginning of the nineteenth century, formalist women organized benevolent societies to support the functions of the church. Through sewing circles, cent societies, and prayer meetings, pious women raised funds to support missionaries, send young men to seminary, pay for the distribution of Bibles, and similar religious causes. By the 1820s such female-led benevolent organizations, with their domain confined to essentially womanly religious concerns and their activities closely tied to the church, were common in Northern formalist congregations. But in communities like Rochester, New York, Finney's perfectionist message encouraged evangelical women to move beyond traditionally female activities. Female converts, infused with the Holy Spirit, fended off comments regarding their proper "sphere," bemoaned their critics' lack of religious fervor, and launched into moral reform. In Rochester formal evangelical women created the Female Charitable Society to aid the poor, the Female Moral Reform Society to redeem prostitutes, the Rochester Orphan Asylum Association to rescue the parentless, and the Female Anti-Slavery Society to destroy the peculiar institution.

Not every community was as receptive to such public activism as was Rochester. In many locales male traditionalists worked to keep women from moving into positions of religious and political leadership. Generally the formalist clergy were committed to a hierarchical view of society with themselves at the top. They often cited St. Paul's injunctions— "Let all things be done decently and in order" and "Let your women keep silence in the churches: for it is not permitted unto them to speak." Consequently most formalist clergy supported women's fund raising for benevolence and tolerated efforts to promote domestic spirituality through maternal associations, but were opposed to female spiritual leadership in public settings. In 1827 conservative revivalists criticized Charles Finney for allowing women to pray and testify in promiscuous, or mixed, worship services. Five years later the Presbyterian General Assembly sided with Finney's critics, stating, "To teach and exhort, or to lead in prayer, in public and promiscuous assemblies, is clearly forbidden to women in the Holy Oracles." Formalist ministers continued to oppose public religious roles for women at mid-century. One cleric walked out of a mixed assembly that was to be addressed by a woman, "declaring that he would as soon rob a hen-roost as remain there and hear a woman speak in public."

The intransigence of the formal evangelical clergy created a crisis for perfectionist women who sought a public arena for their Christian devotion. Inevitably the two groups came into conflict. In 1837 the Massachusetts Congregational clergy, in response to the New England speaking tour of Quaker abolitionists Sarah and Angelina Grimké, condemned female activists who addressed mixed audiences. Sarah Grimké fired back, stating that Jesus defined "the duties of his followers...without any reference to sex or condition [and therefore] Men and women were CREATED EQUAL! They are both moral and accountable beings, and whatever is *right* for a man to do, is *right* for a woman to do." Formalist women seeking a broader social role were faced with a difficult choice: submit to male authority and return to their "proper" place, or join William Lloyd Garrison, Quakers, and others who criticized the formalist clergy. When Oberlin graduate Lucy Stone heard the Grimkés condemned from the pulpit of her Congregational church, she turned against the orthodox church and joined the Garrisonians. From 1837 on, the most effective proponents of women's rights were generally Quakers, nonevangelicals, and ex-formalists who freed themselves from traditional biblical interpretation. In general the formalist emphasis on order that propelled perfectionist women toward organized social reform also worked against women: formalist clergy cited biblical commands for "order" to keep religious females within their "proper sphere."

Internal conflicts over the proper role of women did not shake the confidence of more traditional formalist men and women: whether they relied on church discipline or Finneyite perfectionism to enforce separation from "the world," formal evangelicals believed their orderly Christian faith was best. As a result they looked down on the other two evangelical groups. Horace Bushnell spoke for many elite Easterners when he described the religion of the West (which was, in essence, the religion of the Methodists, Baptists, and Disciples of Christ) as having occasional outbursts "of overwrought feeling or fanatical zeal," and afflicted by "low superstitions...a regarding of dreams, a faith in the presentation of scripture texts, in apparitions and visions, perhaps also in necromancy." Formal evangelical criticism of African American Christianity was even more condemning. A teacher sent south after the Civil War by the American Missionary Association (predominantly a Congregational agency) to instruct ex-slaves described slave religion as a "mass of religious rubbish" that was merely "effervescence of emotional feeling, with very little understanding of even the first elementary principles of the Gospel."

Antiformal evangelicals placed much more emphasis than the formalists on the congregation's role in fostering personal holiness. In the Presbyterian, Episcopalian, and even Congregational churches, the local church was simply an auxiliary within a national system of discipline. Lower-class whites, however, were generally suspicious of national organizations and often questioned their own denominational agencies. Antiformalism was strongest in less commercialized areas where the cult of individualism had not undercut traditional authority. In the South and West individuals were important but not autonomous; they were reined in by the expectations of family and community.

Antiformalists thus emphasized local congregational autonomy and local values in applying behavioral sanctions. The Baptists and Disciples were congregational in polity which meant that members of the local church voted on the defendant's guilt or innocence; there was no higher court of appeal. By contrast, clergy had more power within the Methodist process. Once informed by lay class leaders, they could unilaterally remove flagrant violators. Unhappy Methodists could appeal their cases to the General Conference. But as long as Methodist clergy were circuit riders, obviously men of the people, members did not resent their authority, and appeals to higher powers were rare.

In all three antiformalist groups the local congregation was the chief enforcer of evangelical standards. Discipline was forceful and rigorous, biblical injunctions and church rules were interpreted literally, and members were monitored carefully to keep the world at bay.

Baptists, Methodists, and Disciples worried much about worldliness, particularly when they saw other evangelicals succumb to the lure of status and position. Antiformalists believed that excess wealth promoted worldly values and behavior. A contributor to the Methodist *Southern Christian Advocate* argued "that a church or congregation which is composed mainly of rich men, has more of worldly-mindedness and the pomp and show of earth about it, and less of the vital energy of Christianity within it, than societies which are not so wealthy, and who possess but little of the luxuries of life."

In order to protect themselves from imitating the "coldness" of formalist "heathen churches" (and Methodist and Baptist congregations in the urban North that copied formalist practices), the majority of antiformalists condemned a series of "worldly" innovations. They disapproved of the renting of church pews because they were afraid that wealthy people, who paid more money to obtain pews in the front, would gain disproportionate influence. Musical instruments were condemned as old-fashioned Methodists objected to having "piano thumpers," "fiddling Christians," and "catgut scrapers" participate in services. The Disciples shared these sentiments and banned all musical instruments throughout the denomination. Choirs were also seen as an abomination. Some disliked choirs because they forced the congregation to turn their rear parts to the pulpit so they could hear the music coming from the back of the church. Others hated choirs because professional singers had a reputation for Sabbath desecration, playing cards, and dancing.

But pews, instruments, and choirs were only the symptoms of worldliness; the presence of those who loved money more than God was the cause. So antiformalists strengthened barriers against wealthy ostentation and the sin of pride. Some antiformalists added rituals that the affluent would be unwilling to observe. In 1831 Alabama's Mud Creek Baptist Association declared "feet-washing" to be an ordinance. This practice was modeled after Jesus' washing his disciples' feet and his command for his followers to do likewise. This ritual was an ideal way to keep the well-to-do out of antiformalist churches because few proud and secularized evangelicals would succumb to washing someone else's feet, particularly if the appendages in question belonged to an infrequently bathed frontiersman.

Social pressure was a more common method of avoiding secularization. Worldliness stemmed not so much from having money as from the pride that accompanied wealth. When the affluent displayed their finery to show they were better than others, this sin of ostentation went directly against the Christian message of equality and violated antiformal instincts. Methodist circuit rider Peter Cartwright made it abundantly clear that fancy dress had no place in the Kingdom of God when he revealed how, at a camp meeting, two "very fashionably dressed" ladies gave him their gold chains, earrings, and lockets after their conversion, saying, "We have no more use for these idols. If religion is the glorious, good thing you have represented it to be, it throws these idols into eternal shade." Similarly, the Disciples cautioned against pride in dress and adornment. "Ribbands," "rings," "bracelets," "hooped sleeves," "gold, pearls, and costly array" were condemned, particularly when they were purchased simply because "they are costly." Few people were disciplined or expelled because of their love of finery, but antiformalist leaders made it clear, at least until the 1850s, that faithful Christians observed simplicity of dress.

Not all antiformalists believed that avoiding worldliness was the path to piety; others believed the key to sanctification was to receive "the second blessing." While Baptists and Disciples tended to stick to traditionalist discipline, many Methodists turned their attention to Phoebe Palmer's teachings about entire sanctification. Sometimes the doctrine motivated Methodist women to break out of the women's sphere. Women who desired entire sanctification believed God wanted them to serve him totally, even if it meant moving beyond traditional female roles. For instance, Phoebe Palmer not only distributed tracts and led prayer meetings, she helped found the Five Points Mission which offered jobs, food, clothing, and religious guidance to New York City's poor. Throughout the 1850s other Methodist women were actively involved in helping young delinquents, African American orphans, and the deaf.

Even though antiformalist women entered large-scale benevolence later than formalist women, they made faster progress than their formalist sisters in attaining positions of religious leadership. Antiformalists had long contended that those who spoke "in the Spirit" had greater authority than those who merely had human credentials. Therefore, women who "had the gift" had to be respected. Furthermore, unlike formal evangelicals who used theological education to demark the clergy from the laity, antiformalists blurred the distinction between pastor and parishioner. Methodist class leaders and exhorters filled the middle ground between circuit rider and worshipers. Baptist laymen became preachers by a vote of their local congregation. Because of the fuzzy line between clergy and laity, antiformalist women had more freedom "to testify," "to exhort," and "to preach" than did formalist women. In early nineteenth-century New York Martha Howell and Deborah Pierce worked as itinerant Baptist lay preachers, the latter justifying her activities in a pamphlet entitled "A Scriptural Vindication of Female Preaching, Prophesying, and Exhortation." Methodist women also took advantage of their relative freedom. Females preached in the Methodist Episcopal church as early as the 1820s, and in the Methodist Protestant Church, women like Hannah Pierce Reeves sometimes served as itinerants in Western conferences when there was an inadequate supply of male circuit riders.

Phoebe Palmer's career gave antiformalist female preaching an enormous boost when some antiformalist ministers wanted to keep women from speaking publicly. Palmer responded by writing a 421-page treatise, *The Promise of the Father,* which argued that the gifts of the Spirit—prayer, prophesy, and preaching—were given equally to men and women. Palmer continued by arguing that women could ably serve in both legislative halls and church conventions. Finally she questioned the entire concept of ordination and contended, in true antiformalist fashion, that ordination was man-made, unscriptural, and a departure from the New Testament command for every Christian to preach the gospel. Other women, infused with the spirit of Wesleyan perfectionism, followed Palmer's example and testified to the second blessing. Soon no good Methodist would deny the right of a woman to speak "as the Holy Spirit led her." On one occasion, when a Presbyterian minister questioned the right of a Methodist woman to speak, a camp meeting preacher came to her defense: "She may—she will speak for the cross. We will listen to her testimony and profit from her experience. But not alone from potency of influence or dignity of her nature, but because of Pentecost."

Like the formalists, antiformal evangelicals believed their version of the faith to be superior to all others. Baptists, Methodists, and Disciples not only viewed formalist denominations as too secular and worldly but also questioned the piety of black evangelicals. A white Baptist wrote to the *Religious Herald* criticizing the practice of admitting "coloured members [who] are ignorant, superstitious, and fanatical." Others complained about black church members who lied, stole, or committed adultery. From the 1830s on, Southern whites increasingly moved from biracial churches to preferring that blacks worship by themselves under white supervision. In the end, white antiformalists found African American evangelicalism to be unacceptable on two counts: it contained African elements, and its advocates were black.

The great frustration of African American evangelicals was that they desired lives of holiness and purity, but the slave system kept them from living the evangelical ethic. According to the middle-class cult of true womanhood, women were to define themselves through submission, piety, purity, and domesticity. Under slavery all four values were either perverted or denied. As we have seen earlier, true African American piety involved great risks. Harriet Jacobs, a runaway slave, revealed in her autobiography how the ideal of submitting to male authority was twisted under the system of bondage as owners forced slave women to yield to their lecherous advances. In an appeal to Northern women, Jacobs also revealed how purity and domesticity were denied under slavery.

> O, ye happy women, whose purity has been sheltered from childhood, who have been free to choose the objects

of your affection, whose homes are protected by law, do
not judge the poor desolate slave girl too severely! If
slavery had been abolished, I, also, could have married
the man of my choice; I could have had a home shielded
by the laws; and I should have been spared the painful
task of confessing what I am now about to relate; but all
my prospects had been blighted by slavery. I wanted to
keep myself pure; and, under the most adverse circumstances, I tried hard to preserve my self-respect; but
I was struggling alone in the powerful grasp of the
demon Slavery; and the monster proved too strong
for me.

In the North, African American evangelical women were
more open in pursuing personal holiness. The desire of
black women "to do good" was shaped not by Finneyite or
Wesleyan perfectionism but by a desire shared by both black
men and women to strengthen the black community and to
destroy slavery. Thus African American women who crossed
into the public sphere received less opposition from black
men than white evangelical women experienced from white
men. Not only did black women work on local benevolence,
but many became preachers and exhorters. Jarena Lee was
the African Methodist Episcopal denomination's first female
preacher. Other female evangelists, including Julia Foote and
Juliann Jane Tillman, played a major role in expanding
AME membership before the Civil War. Some female preachers, like Zilpha Elaw, free-lanced, preaching wherever they
believed the Spirit led them. But black female activism did
not stop with benevolence and preaching: many evangelical
women could not rest until they had rescued their brothers
and sisters from the snares of bondage. Some women fought
slavery from the domestic sphere, protecting runaways in
their homes and churches. Others fought the peculiar insti-

tution from the public sphere. In 1832 Maria Stewart, a member of Boston's African Baptist Church, orated against slavery before the "Afric-American Female Intelligence Society." In the 1840s and 1850s Sojourner Truth (AMEZ), who responded to a heavenly vision by becoming an abolitionist lecturer, traveled throughout the North, "testifyin' agin concerning the wickedness of this 'ere people." Not surprisingly, both Stewart and Truth also became outspoken women's rights advocates.

Just as female slaves realized it was impossible to pursue true womanhood, enslaved men found the nineteenth-century ideal of manhood to be beyond their grasp. Freedom to operate in the public sphere, financial independence, and the ability to protect one's family from harm were all denied to bondsmen. Not only were they denied public political rights, but plantation slaves needed passes to go to town for supplies, to visit nearby relatives, or to attend any errand off the estate. One of the most troubling aspects of slave marriage was the inability of black men to protect family members from white abuse. The vast majority preferred to be married to someone from a different plantation so they would not have to see their wives suffer. John Anderson related, "I did not want to marry a girl belonging to my own place, because I knew I could not bear to see her ill-treated." Moses Grandy concurred when he wrote, "No colored man wishes to live at the house where his wife lives, for he has to endure the continual misery of seeing her flogged and abused, without daring to say a word in her defence." As with the women, enslaved men were kept from living the evangelical ethic. This denial of personal fulfillment put slave evangelicals in a difficult position. How could they attempt to live a just and holy life when slavery frustrated their ability to conduct themselves righteously?

One approach was to try to obey the Ten Commandments and fulfill evangelical expectations as best they could. By scrupulously following the Ten Commandments and living lives beyond reproach, African American evangelicals refuted the owner-encouraged stereotypes, maintained their dignity, and claimed moral superiority over the slaveholding class.

Most black evangelicals took a second approach and recognized that the Ten Commandments could not be followed literally under slavery. African trickster tales, which showed how the weak could outwit the powerful, were more practical guides to everyday behavior. Stealing food was necessary to fight the ravages of malnutrition, and running away was often the only way to escape severe beatings or even death. When whites came to all-black churches and demanded that slaves be prosecuted for theft and running away, African American parishioners refused to cooperate. Presbyterian missionary Charles Colcock Jones noted that "members of the same church are sacredly bound by their religion not to reveal each other's sins, for that would be backbiting and injuring the brotherhood." A South Carolinian wrote, "It was a rule among the members of these [slave religious] societies, rigidly enforced, never to divulge the secret of stealing; to do so brought dire punishment upon the informer."

As things stood, black evangelicals had little reason for loyalty to earth; instead they were part of God's heavenly kingdom. Slaves sometimes sang:

This world is not my home.
This world is not my home.
This world's a howling wilderness,
This world is not my home.

Even more than white evangelicals, African American believers saw themselves as separate from the world.

African American evangelicals condemned "the world" of Southern slaveholders and focused particular criticism on hypocritical white evangelicals who profited from the peculiar institution. Frequently slaves made remarks about their masters' future damnation. One slave told her mistress, "You no holy. We be holy. You in no state of salvation." Others rejoiced when their mistress died, saying "Old God damn son-of-a-bitch, she gone on down to hell." Some blacks went so far as to believe that white people would not be in heaven. Frederick Douglass summarized black estimates of white Southern Christianity: "I love the pure, peaceable, and impartial Christianity of Christ: I therefore hate the corrupt, slaveholding [,] women-whipping, cradle-plundering, partial and hypocritical Christianity of this land." In the final analysis, Douglass said, "the religion of the south is a mere covering for the most horrid crimes."

Black evangelicals drew the sharpest line between themselves and the hypocritical faith of most Southern whites, yet it was not the only barrier against the world. African American believers also separated themselves from African religious ideas that ran counter to evangelical teaching. By the early nineteenth century the remnants of African religious practice were known as conjure or hoodoo.* Most large plantations had at least one priest-practitioner who claimed to use the forces of nature to work good or evil, and

*Historians distinguish between "voodoo," which was a complete religious system (with institutions, rituals, and a complete theology), and "hoodoo," which was a series of religious beliefs and practices that existed after the larger African religious system had disappeared. Many nineteenth-century African Americans used the two terms interchangeably.

to employ herbs, roots, and spells to foster love, cure the sick, or protect one from harm. Black evangelicals opposed African spirit-based religion. Slave testimonials indicate they believed Christians had no business dabbling in hoodoo. Some blacks dismissed conjure outright. Martha Colquitt remembered: "Us all de time heard folkses talkin' about voodoo, but my grandma was powerful religious, and her and Ma tell us chillen voodoo was a no 'count doin' of de devil, and Christians was never to pay it no attention." While black evangelicals opposed African religious beliefs, they sometimes accepted African practices after separating the practice from its non-Christian origins. After professing how God showed him "There ain't no such thing as conjurers," one believer continued, "I believe in root-doctors because, after all, we must depend upon some form of root or weed to cure the sick."

Similarly, black evangelicals opposed violins and fiddles because they played important roles in African religious ceremonies. The one-string violin was used in the old Mali Empire to call up the ancestral spirits. In America violins and fiddles were used for the same purpose. Not surprisingly, Methodist missionaries were appalled by this practice and sought to ban them from plantations. Upon conversion many blacks gave up fiddle-playing, believing it to be a worldly, non-Christian activity. One recalled his preconversion state: "I loved to drink; I loved to play the fiddle and I don't believe anyone can be a good devout Christian and do these things." Ex-slave Willis Winn concurred: "When I joined the church, I burned my fiddle up."

Dancing was another practice that separated black Christians from the African "world." Like fiddle-playing, dance played an integral part in African religious ceremonies, the climax coming when divinities or the living dead seized the

dancers and "danced" them before the assembled community. Evangelicals, however, condemned all dancing (except
in its Christianized form when participants were seized by
the Holy Ghost). Nineteenth-century black conversion narratives reveal that many African Americans saw the choice
being between God and the dance floor. One ex-slave confessed, "I was a great dancer when I grew up and in spite of
my praying I went to dances. One night I went to a dance
but I didn't feel right and, strange to say, every time I got on
the floor to dance a round, the fiddle-string would break.
All of a sudden while I was in my place ready to dance I
heard a voice on the inside that said, 'Do you remember the
promise you made to me?'" Guilt feelings overwhelmed the
dancer, who then had a dramatic conversion. As music was
too central to black culture to be abandoned, evangelicals
modified dance (by forbidding the crossing of feet) and
created the ring shout. Thus every Saturday night the
converted celebrated God's grace by "shouting" at the praise-
house while worldings danced the evening away in the
quarters. Both drew on African tradition, yet the line
between the church and the world was clearly drawn.

Like other antebellum evangelicals, African Americans
sought to live a just and holy life by making war on the
world, the flesh, and the devil. But their battle was more
fierce than that of white evangelicals. Drawing on African
thought patterns, black evangelicals saw Satan in intensely
personal terms, a fiend who sought to destroy their souls.
Instead of battling one "world," they fought both against the
world of hypocritical slaveholders and the world of the
conjurers. In each case they drew the line of separation as
sharply as they could. With lines against the world doubly
drawn, and without access to secularizing wealth, the black
church maintained itself as a community set apart. After the

Civil War, when "invisible" slave congregations became "visible" by officially organizing, the black evangelical church continued to be a powerful institution, giving hope and direction to its members.

The evangelical desire to improve one's spiritual life paralleled a general American desire to improve the quality of one's life. Rather than focusing on justice and holiness, other reformers were more concerned with being healthy and happy. By mid-century, perfectionism appeared in secular as well as religious forms as reformers tried to rid themselves of a variety of ills. These problem-solving efforts took both individualistic and communitarian forms.

Many antebellum Americans were more concerned about their bodies than their souls. Nor did America lack for volunteers willing to guide the nation toward physical perfection. Sylvester Graham, a Presbyterian minister and temperance lecturer, contended that all diseases came from stomach irritation. The solution, according to Graham, was a high-fiber diet which included bran breads, fruit, and vegetables and excluded all stimulants—coffee, tea, alcohol, spices, and meat. The Graham program was comprehensive and advised people on clothing, exercise, and ventilation. In addition, Graham warned against excessive sex: "too frequently repeated [it] cannot fail to produce the most terrible effects." In essence Graham imposed order on his followers' physical lives, promising that self-discipline over one's body was essential to well-being.

While the Grahamites viewed proper diet as essential to good health, Mary Gove Nichols saw salvation in water. Nichols was a leading advocate of hydropathy, a method of cleansing and healing the body by frequently drinking and bathing in water. By 1862 seventy resorts devoted to the

method were spread across the country as thousands of
Americans sought to correct their ailments through the
water cure.

Others sought happiness by consulting a new "science"
called phrenology. Practitioners claimed the ability to determine anyone's personality by surveying the shape of his or
her cranium. Believing that the brain contained thirty-seven
"faculties," that the strength of each faculty was equal to the
size of the "organ" that contained it, and that the skull's
shape reflected the size of the various organs, phrenologists
evaluated personality traits by measuring protrusions and
indentations on the skull's surface. Once a personality profile
had been created, the practitioner advised clients on everything from prospective mates to finding employment suited
to their personalities. As Americans gradually moved away
from spiritual to secular advisers, phrenologists stood mid-
way between ministers and psychologists.

Utopian reformers believed that the quality of life could
be perfected by restructuring the local community. Much
like traditionalist church leaders who believed that personal
holiness was fostered by strong group identity and strict
discipline, utopian leaders believed that social perfection
could be achieved only by withdrawing into a self-governing
society that operated on principles much different from the
surrounding world. One of the most radical experiments, the
Oneida Community, had evangelical roots. Oneida's founder,
John Humphrey Noyes, was converted in 1831 and soon
afterward entered the Yale Divinity School. While at Yale he
pushed the concept of perfectionism to new extremes by
contending that true Christians were incapable of all sin.
Believing that Christ intended his followers to have all
things in common (including property and sexual partners),
Noyes founded a perfectionist community in western New

York in 1848. While Oneida did not redeem America by ushering in a new social order, the community did turn a sizable profit, and by 1875 it had accumulated a half-million dollars in assets. Ultimately monogamous marriage conquered Noyes's system of "complex marriage," and the community disbanded in 1881.

Less radical than Oneida, Hopedale and Brook Farm also tried to perfect American life by offering a communitarian alternative. Adin Ballou, a Universalist minister, modeled Hopedale after the joint stock company. Residents worked together on farming and other commercial projects, owned shares in the enterprise, and were rewarded with dividends according to the number of shares purchased. Unfortunately for this model "Christian Republic," two of its members bought up three-fourths of the shares and disbanded the project in 1856. Brook Farm was organized much like Hopedale but was populated by individualistic intellectuals who were much better at organizing creative schools and reporting their exploits to the public than they were at turning a profit. After numerous attempts at reorganization, and after the uninsured main building was destroyed by fire, Brook Farm limped along for a few years until its remaining property was sold in 1849.

While Oneida, Hopedale, and Brook Farm were inspired by religious and humanitarian idealism, other communities were based on secular economic theories. Robert Owen rejected traditional religion, instead seeking to improve American lives by the "science of man." Owen believed that human character was shaped by its surroundings, and human behavior could therefore be redesigned by changing the environment. Two ideas were central to Owen's social reorganization: all people were to "be equal in their condition," and cooperation was to replace the American "competitive system." By eliminating the capitalist environment Owen hoped to create new human beings who put the good of the whole over personal gratification. In the mid-1820s Owen tried to implement his theories by founding a socialist community at New Harmony, Indiana. But the project suffered due to overcrowding, individualistic residents, and a lack of leadership (Owen was often traveling on the east coast and in England to promote the enterprise). The experiment was dissolved in 1827.

In the 1840s Albert Brisbane tried a new approach to reorganizing the American community. Like Owen, he looked to economics and other secular theories of human behavior for inspiration. Brisbane modeled much of his thinking on the theories of Charles Fourier, who believed communities could be organized into "phalanxes" of fifteen hundred to eighteen hundred people. All residents would live in a "phalanstry," a carefully designed building that structured and organized all of the community's activities. Using the best of nineteenth-century psychology, Brisbane tried to make work pleasurable by matching tasks to individual personality types. Brisbane and other Fourierists established twenty-eight communities across the United States, the longest lasting being the North American Phalanx in New Jersey. Even though the New Jersey experiment was financially successful, enthusiasm eventually waned, and the phalanx was dissolved in 1856.

The evangelical drive to perfect their own lives was part of a larger American effort to improve the quality of human experience. Some efforts focused on the body, others on the mind, still others on reorganizing community life. But all these efforts at individual and community-level reform paled in comparison with evangelical efforts to change the structure of America. When evangelicals turned outward to redeem the nation, hardly an American institution remained unaffected.

4

God's Chosen People

LIKE OTHER ASPECTS of evangelical thinking, the idea that Americans were God's chosen people began far back in the colonial past. Early in the seventeenth century John Rolfe called Virginia's colonists "a peculiar people, marked and chosen by the hand of God." John Winthrop, the foremost political leader in Massachusetts Bay from the organization of the English expedition in 1629 until his death in 1649, believed that God had called the Puritans on an errand into the wilderness, to be a Holy Nation and an example to the entire world. In Winthrop's words, the Puritan colony was to "be as a City upon a Hill [as] the eyes of all people are upon us." In Winthrop's view God was obligated to bring prosperity to Massachusetts only to the degree the Puritans followed divine commandments. As a result, any individual's sin endangered the colony's survival, and to protect itself the Bay Colony wove Old Testament law into its legal code. Ultimately Puritan covenant theology meant that religious and political leaders had to work together to ensure that all colonists pursued personal holiness.

The concept that Massachusetts was God's New Israel flourished in the Bay Colony during the early colonial period. When Puritan settlement spread beyond Massachusetts's borders, the concept evolved into a covenant between

God and New England. By the time of the American
Revolution many argued that the thirteen British colonies
were God's chosen people. By the mid-nineteenth century
the concept of America's divine role was securely planted in
the nation's consciousness. In 1850 Herman Melville wrote:
"We Americans are the peculiar, chosen people—the Israel
of our time; we bear the ark of the liberties of the world....
God has predestined, mankind expects, great things from
our race; and great things we feel in our souls. The rest of
the nations must soon be in our rear. We are the pioneers of
the world; the advance-guard, sent on through the wilderness of untried things, to break a new path in the New
World that is ours."

Most antebellum evangelicals agreed that God's favored
people were found in America. But they differed in interpreting this concept. Once again social location was crucial as
formalists emphasized the national covenant, antiformalists
gravitated toward Manifest Destiny, and African Americans
reinterpreted the New Israel theme in light of slavery.

Formal evangelicals stressed the Puritan concept that God
had a covenant with his chosen people in which he pledged
to bless them in direct proportion to their faithfulness.
Americans were God's chosen people, but such a position
entailed risks as well as rewards. If the United States was not
righteous, God might strike down this nation just as he
allowed Assyria, Babylon, and Rome to conquer ancient
Israel. Therefore America must obey divine law, and even
the unconverted must live godly lives. Righteousness could
not be trusted to individuals and to congregations alone but
had to be institutionalized within the national fabric. Thus
formalists created organizations to correct injustice and
reduce human suffering, ranging from the American Anti-

Slavery Society to the National Truss Society for the Relief of the Ruptured Poor. When it became clear that voluntary agencies by themselves could not insure America's goodness, formalists sought to mandate righteousness through state and national laws such as prohibition. Because they believed God to be fundamentally concerned with justice, formalists were reluctant to support Manifest Destiny which involved taking land that belonged to others and which encouraged the expansion of slavery.

Antiformal evangelicals also believed Americans were God's anointed, but they focused more on God's gift of land than on covenantal obligations. Instead of worrying about God's justice, antiformalists generally spoke of America in Edenic terms, often referring to God's invitation to Adam and Eve—"Be fruitful, and multiply, and replenish the earth, and subdue it." Daniel S. Dickinson echoed this theme before the Senate in 1848: "We [have not] yet fulfilled the destiny allotted to us. New territory is spread out for us to subdue and fertilize; new races are presented for us to civilize, educate and absorb; new triumphs for us to achieve for the cause of freedom." Manifest Destiny was a hallowed concept among antiformalists. Stephen A. Douglas, who had Baptist sympathies, and James K. Polk, a Methodist, were two of the doctrine's greatest proponents. Not surprisingly, support for expansion was strongest in the lower Midwest and in the South, regions which would benefit most by westward growth and which, not coincidentally, were dominated by Baptists and Methodists.

African Americans were not impressed with white claims to be God's chosen people. According to white formalists, God's favor depended on "American justice." African Americans believed that the words "American" and "justice" could never fit together as long as slavery existed within the nation's borders. White antiformalists believed Manifest Destiny helped expand freedom westward. Blacks considered this idea to be a patent lie, for in reality expansion only enlarged the territory of human bondage. Yet the concept of the New Israel had tremendous meaning for black Americans as they appropriated the concept for themselves. Black evangelicals preferred the Old Testament and favored the story of the Exodus most of all. African American believers maintained that they were the chosen people and that God would liberate them from white America (Egypt). Spirituals commonly identified the singers as "de people of de Lord," "We are the people of God," and "I'm born of God, I know I am." Blacks also reversed the image of Washington, the white "Moses." According to slave folklore, George Washington's last plea on his deathbed was to "forever keep the niggers down." By contrast, during and after the Civil War, Lincoln's reputation rose to Mosaic proportions. According to slave legend, the Great Emancipator visited Southern plantations before the Great Conflict in order to see slavery firsthand and to go "all through de country just a-rantin' an' a-preachin' about us being his black brothers."

The three social groups also had different strategies for redeeming the nation from its imperfect state and for bringing the Kingdom of God to America. Formalists sought to establish a holy order through voluntarism and political action in the public sphere. While they believed private righteousness was important, personal holiness was not sufficient to cure all social ills. Antiformalists believed the nation could be redeemed from vice through personal conversion, the guidance of the local church, and (to a limited degree) benevolence by denominational societies. They were wary of nondenominational voluntary societies and generally shunned the use of law to force people into higher standards of behavior. African American evangelicals wanted black believers to uphold the Ten Commandments and other aspects of the evangelical ideal. But black evangelicals realized they would make little progress in promoting ideal behavior until the evil of slavery was eliminated. How could even white Southerners truly understand the gospel as long as slavery corrupted white souls and encouraged church members to commit diabolical acts? For black evangelicals, destroying slavery was the key to redeeming both black and white America.

A number of issues demonstrate how formal, antiformal, and black evangelicals approached public morality differently. But three issues—the observance of the Sabbath, the use of alcohol, and the problem of slavery—dominated antebellum discourse and aptly illustrate the divisions among evangelicals.

Evangelicals considered Sabbath observance one of their pietistic duties. Methodist James Finley refused to join his fellows in Sunday hunting and fishing because he was brought up to keep the Sabbath holy. Lyman Beecher was so strict in his observance that his children were not allowed to play with their toys on Sunday. In 1831 Tocqueville was amazed that "Boston on Sunday has, literally, the appearance of a deserted town."

In 1810 Congress passed a law requiring postmasters to open their offices every day that letters and packages arrived from outside communities. Because transport lines found it most profitable to operate seven days a week and because the law did not prohibit Sunday activity, mail was delivered to post offices seven days a week. This meant that local offices had to distribute mail to customers for at least an hour every Sunday. The post office was the perfect place for nonchurch-

goers to spend their Sundays away from worship. Even the
pious were affected, as evangelical wives were annoyed when
their husbands walked out of Sunday services as soon as they
heard the stagecoach clatter into town with the day's mail.
Formal evangelicals were distraught over government-spon-
sored Sabbath desecration. The Presbyterian General Assembly warned in 1812 that if Congress failed to repent,
"our nation" might suffer "divine displeasure." In 1814
Presbyterians and Congregationalists mounted a joint petition drive to encourage Congress to reverse the Sunday mail
law. These efforts collapsed by 1817, and Sabbatarianism lay
dormant for almost a decade.

The campaign to end Sunday mail delivery began anew in
1826. Congress had renewed the objectionable postal law in
1825, and transportation had improved greatly since the end
of the War of 1812. As efficient transportation expanded
across the country, so did the Sabbath violations that came
with Sunday mail delivery. Political action seemed necessary
because the traditional methods of using church discipline
with members and persuasion with nonmembers were fail-
ing. As long as there was a commercial advantage to getting
news at the post office each Sunday, men tended to ignore
church opinion and follow the dictates of their pocketbooks.
Sabbatarians also had new reason for hope. Formal evangelicals had experienced a series of revivals in a number of
Northeastern cities and villages which encouraged the faithful and swelled membership rolls. Thus a heightened sense
of danger stemming from "a trampling of the laws of God,"
plus renewed formal evangelical vigor, combined to create a
second, stronger Sabbatarian movement.

As before, Congregationalists and Presbyterians led the
second drive to end Sunday mail transport and delivery.
Like the first campaign, the second crusade drew heavily on

formalist thinking regarding the national covenant. "While the arm of Jehovah is lifted for our defence, no enemy can subdue us," the Sabbatarians declared. "But if the supreme Legislature of this Union...makes it necessary to violate *the command of God,* his justice will demand that adequate punishment be inflicted on our common country." This time, however, the campaign was better organized and employed a variety of methods to undo the postal law.

Sabbatarians began their assault by applying economic pressure to induce stagecoach, steamboat, and canal packet lines to abandon all Sunday delivery, which would relieve post offices of the obligation to open on Sundays. In 1826 the Presbyterian General Assembly urged its members to boycott any company operating seven days a week. For such a boycott to be successful, formalist businessmen had to have alternative transportation that operated only six days a week. In 1827 Josiah Bissel, a Presbyterian elder and a successful Rochester merchant, founded a Sabbath-keeping transport company—the Pioneer Line—that ran stagecoaches and canal packets between Albany and Buffalo, New York. When the new venture opened for business it was probably the best-equipped transportation company in the nation and promised to move people and goods faster in six days than its chief competitor—the Old Line Mail—could move them in seven.

The second step was to raise public consciousness about the Sabbath. If evangelicals were not sufficiently aroused to use the Pioneer Line, efforts to provide a non-Sabbath-breaking transportation system were doomed. In 1828 Bissel played a leading role in organizing the General Union for the Promotion of the Christian Sabbath. To join, one had to pledge to keep the Sabbath and to boycott all transport companies that operated seven days a week. The General

Union cleverly sought to broaden its moralistic base by appealing to others' economic interests. To the working poor General Union propagandists argued that laborers had a God-given right to a day of rest. To merchants they contended that the right to boycott was an essential property right. Copying the methods of the Tract and Bible societies already in existence, the General Union used modern printing technology to spread 100,000 copies of their message across the country.

The culminating step was to convince Congress to ban the conveying of mail and the opening of post offices on Sundays. Like the benevolent societies before them, the General Union organized local auxiliaries and encouraged members to petition Congress for a change in the postal law. The petitioners generally argued on the basis of republican theory and constitutional law. Virtue was necessary for a republic's survival, said the Sabbatarians, and Sunday mail delivery ought to be stopped because it undercut worship, thus undermining the piety and virtue of the American people. Furthermore, contended the petitioners, the postal code was unconstitutional because it kept pious postmasters from attending church on Sunday, thus depriving them of the free exercise of religion guaranteed by the First Amendment. By May 1831 more than nine hundred petitions reached Congress, some of which had as many as seven thousand signatures.

While Sabbatarians sought to overturn the 1825 postal statute, antiformalists, particularly those in the Southern and Western states, fought bitterly against any changes in Sunday delivery laws. Part of the anti-Sabbatarian response was economic. The Northeastern and mid-Atlantic states received news about European markets first. The time lag before this news reached the West and South handicapped merchants there because they could not respond quickly to changes in European demand. Interrupting mail transport once a week would only aggravate the situation and could delay information sent to New Orleans by an additional three days. Not surprisingly, Sabbatarian support reflected economic realities: 75 percent of the petitions came from New England and the mid-Atlantic states, only 9 percent came from the Northwestern states, and 5 percent from the Southwestern states.

Economic concerns were secondary to antiformal evangelical fears over the combining of church and state. Most Methodists, Baptists, and "Christians" viewed the drive to purify the Sabbath as one more attempt by "Presbygationalists" to foist their religious views on the American public. The staunch Baptist Senator Richard M. Johnson of Kentucky, chairman of the Committee on the Post Office and Post Roads, declared that "extensive religious combinations to effect a political object are . . . always dangerous," and that Congress was not a "proper tribunal" to establish the "laws of God." While a majority of Americans agreed that Sunday was the Lord's Day, Johnson added, congressional rulings based on such sentiments violated the rights of Jews and Christian sects that observed the seventh day. In true antiformalist fashion, Johnson held that the real answer to Sunday transgressions was for Christians to "appeal exclusively to the great Lawgiver of the universe to aid them in making men better, in correcting their practices by purifying their hearts." Fellow Baptist John Leland ridiculed the Sabbatarian cause, suggesting that formalists were seeking to enforce an eleventh commandment to "Remember the first day of the week, and keep it hypocritically." Disciples leaders Alexander Campbell and Barton Stone opposed the Sabbath crusade because it was the first step toward creating a

national church and because it discriminated against those
who worshiped God on Saturday.

The battle between formal and antiformal evangelicals
over the Sabbath came to a surprisingly rapid conclusion.
Economically the Pioneer Line lost its battle against the Old
Line Mail and was discontinued. Politically Richard Johnson
articulated the position of the Democratic party. With Johnson chairing the Postal Committee and Democrats controlling the White House and both houses of Congress, Sabbatarians realized they had no chance to reverse the 1825 postal
law. Recognizing its cause as hopeless, the General Union for
the Promotion of the Christian Sabbath disbanded in May
1832.

The temperance movement addressed a more divisive problem in American society—the growing use and abuse of
alcohol. In the early nineteenth century Protestant clergymen
bemoaned the nation's drinking habits, arguing that intemperance was spreading "like the plague" throughout the
country and that soon the United States would be "a nation
of drunkards." These cries of alarm were more than ministerial hysteria: between 1800 and 1830 the annual consumption
of alcohol steadily rose until it surpassed five gallons per
capita. Whiskey was the most popular intoxicant partly
because of its availability and partly because it was 45
percent alcohol (90 proof) and packed a considerable punch.
With whiskey leading the way, American per capita alcohol
consumption in the first three decades of the nineteenth
century was triple what the national average would be in
1980.

During the 1700s the governing classes were not greatly
concerned about excessive public drinking since the lower
classes generally deferred to their superiors when tavern

behavior got out of hand. But after the American Revolution working-class deference declined, and the lower classes sought self-determination over drinking behavior. Those who campaigned for public office were expected to "treat" the electorate, a practice so common that one Kentucky politician noted that "the way to men's hearts, is, *down their throats.*" By the early 1800s whiskey was such a common part of everyday life that many fathers began to teach their sons to consume small quantities of liquor when the youngsters were merely a year old.

Economic conditions were equally important in contributing to America's alcohol binge. The early nineteenth-century diet emphasized greasy, fried food—usually corn mush, johnnycakes, and salt pork—over healthier but rarer and more expensive fruits and vegetables. Food was generally bland, and Americans compensated by eating the unappetizing fare quickly, often completing a meal in less than five minutes. Rapid eating required a drink that was disease-free, inexpensive, and widely available, to help each mouthful slide down more easily. Whiskey was the ideal beverage. Water (frequently drawn from polluted streams and contaminated wells) and milk (often bacteria-laden and sometimes poisonous) were dangerous. Coffee, tea, and fermented beverages such as beer and wine were either expensive or of poor quality. By comparison, distilled spirits were extremely inexpensive. Because of poor transportation, Western farmers had to convert their grain into a more valuable and nonperishable commodity before they transported it. By using the latest in still technology a farmer could convert 25 cents' worth of corn into $1.25 in spirits. With such economic enticements, Western farmers flooded the nation with inexpensive, potent whiskey. Any white man, no matter how poor, had enough money to get drunk in the early 1800s.

Evangelical churches wrestled with the problem of growing alcoholism because their members were among the intoxicated. Traditional methods of church discipline usually failed to bring inebriated members into line. In the Northeast excessive drinking made up a small number of discipline cases, but in those instances where drinking was the offense, church trials were generally unsuccessful in producing reformation. Drinking was a more serious problem for Southern and Western churches. These congregations resided in areas where alcohol was produced, where many farmers were engaged in the manufacture and sale of spirits, and where the ethos of honor portrayed heavy drinking as a sign of manliness. Intoxication was the most frequent offense in Southern Presbyterian and Baptist churches and was a common complaint in Southern Methodist fellowships.

Since church discipline alone was unable to stem rising levels of alcohol usage, formal evangelicals organized associations to combat the growing evil. Presbyterians and Congregationalists formed state and local societies early in the nineteenth century, and in 1826 they led the drive to create the American Temperance Society. Not surprisingly, this society received its greatest support from the commercial Northeast where heavy drinking interfered with the values of self-control, punctuality, respect for property, and public order that were essential to the more heavily populated, emerging industrial society. The American Temperance Society emphasized changing drinkers' attitudes. By getting moderate users to pledge to abstain from all distilled spirits (except as a medicine), the ATS encouraged members to control themselves: "Our main object is...to induce all temperate people to continue temperate by practicing total abstinence." The temperance pledge kept moderate drinkers from becoming drunkards and was democratic, voluntary, and individualistic in that people chose abstinence for themselves. In short, this tactic perfectly fit the emerging middleclass personality.

The American Temperance Society used tactics similar to those of the Sabbatarians. While economic pressure was not the centerpiece of its program, temperance reformers publicly accosted merchants who manufactured and sold distilled beverages. The second and most important American Temperance Society strategy was to elevate public consciousness regarding alcohol. Like the American Tract Society, the Temperance Society flooded the nation with inexpensive pamphlets and, like many benevolent groups, founded its own newspaper, the *Journal of Humanity*. Like all benevolent agencies, the national society employed an army of agents to crisscross the nation organizing local auxiliaries and collecting funds. Recognizing that women had raised enormous sums for the tract and mission causes, the ATS encouraged the formation of "ladies" temperance societies. More frequently women joined "male" chapters; during the 1830s females comprised 35 to 60 percent of a typical auxiliary's membership. But the formalist-dominated ATS was obsessed with decorum and warned women that there was to be "no sacrifice of delicacy, no stepping beyond your proper sphere." As a result, most women were not allowed to vote or hold leadership roles in the temperance movement, though some broke with the ATS and organized separate all-female state campaigns in the late 1830s.

Initially, the ATS relied on moral suasion to convince people to abstain from all distilled liquors. This gradualist approach recognized that the chronically intoxicated would never reform and that America would be free of drunkenness only when hardened drinkers had died off. But not all ATS members were willing to restrict themselves to per-

suading moderate drinkers not to drink at all. Some Massachusetts societies moved beyond gradualist moral suasion
and began to push for local control over liquor licenses.
Under the local option plan, each township voted on whether to allow the retail sale of alcohol. Bay State reformers
soon recognized that township-level decisions weren't very
effective, as drinkers in a dry township could easily find a
wet township within riding distance. County-level licensing
appeared to be a better strategy because it allowed a county-
wide dry majority to ban alcohol sales from the entire
county, thus keeping wet townships from licensing liquor
establishments. Despite the efforts of the Massachusetts chapters, however, county-level prohibition was widely violated
by taverns that conducted their usual trade without a license.

By the mid-1830s it was clear that the American Temperance Society had been only partially successful in eliminating
the use of alcohol. At about the same time Finneyite
perfectionism was spreading among formal evangelicals, and
formalist temperance advocates were ready to perfect the
temperance pledge. In 1836 temperance advocates organized
the American Temperance Union, which featured an oath to
abstain from *all* intoxicating beverages, not just from distilled spirits. This teetotal pledge purified evangelicals, since
no liquor entered their bodies. It also purified the movement
by expelling upper-class social drinkers who were ready to
deprive workingmen of their whiskey but were not willing
to give up their own wine. The American Temperance
Union, cleansed from within, was now ready to perfect
America by ridding the country of its drinking problem.

Like the ATS, the American Temperance Union employed a threefold attack. It publicly criticized those in the
liquor trade, whether they sold whiskey, beer, or wine. It
raised public consciousness by rejecting the old pledge and

encouraging citizens to sign the new teetotal pledge. But the Union concentrated its energy on political action. By the late 1830s some temperance advocates turned to statewide prohibition, particularly after the Massachusetts Temperance Union pushed the fifteen-gallon law (which banned the sale of distilled spirits, except for medicinal and mechanical purposes, in quantities less than fifteen gallons) through the state's legislature in 1838. After proliquor forces overturned the Massachusetts law in 1840, advocates of statewide prohibition were relatively quiet for a decade. But in 1851 Congregationalist layman Neal Dow and the Maine Temperance Union successfully lobbied the Maine state legislature to enact a new statewide prohibition statute. The Maine Law authorized search warrants to investigate unlawful liquor sales, mandated that illegal alcohol be seized and destroyed, drastically increased fines on convicted sellers, and required that dealers be sent to prison for three to six months when convicted a third time. The Maine Law appeared to be the ultimate weapon needed to win the war against alcohol. By 1855 twelve other states passed similar legislation and victory appeared close in four more. Unlike the Sabbatarians, temperance advocates convinced a majority of Northerners that the law was a legitimate tool to be used in bringing the Kingdom of God to America.

When prohibitionism reached its zenith in 1855, a great many antiformalists joined formalists in supporting the new regulations. Just the same, prohibitionists were a minority among antiformal evangelicals; the majority believed that Christians were free to drink alcoholic beverages but were not to imbibe to the point of intoxication. Many, but not all, antiformalists voluntarily abstained from using any alcohol. But most viewed this as a personal moral decision that should not be forced upon them by any outside religious or political force.

Most antiformal evangelicals fell into two camps—the first opposed all temperance societies on principle, and the second opposed only societies that promoted prohibition. The smaller group, which opposed all temperance organizations on principle, was strongest in remote, less commercialized, and underindustrialized regions. These antitemperance advocates, who were frequently antimission Baptists, argued that a moderate use of alcohol was a traditional right and that no organization had the authority to tell other folks how to behave. Many antitemperance men were farmers who were accustomed to using a shot of whiskey to keep themselves going from sunrise to sunset and to reinvigorate the body before the next set of chores. For many others, serving liquor was a traditional means of hospitality. Furthermore, many antiformalists had economic reasons for opposing temperance. Rural Baptists and Methodists were often liquor dealers who believed there was nothing inherently wrong with distilled spirits and that turning one's grain into marketable and transportable whiskey was a legitimate way to make a profit. Pointing out that Christ not only drank but *made* wine, antitemperance Baptists and Methodists accused the antiliquor forces of ignoring the Bible's literal statements about Jesus and alcohol. Some congregations went so far as to excommunicate members who took the teetotal pledge or who had joined temperance societies.

While a minority of antiformalists opposed temperance societies, the majority supported them as long as the society promoted voluntary abstinence and did not seek to curtail alcohol use by law. As a result these antiformalists had significant reservations about the American Temperance Society. In Maine, for instance, Baptists and Methodists often viewed temperance as "a federal plot" and refused to join because they wanted "to prevent a union between church and state."

Unlike the formalist-controlled ATS and ATU, the anti-prohibitionist Washingtonian movement (and its successors, the Rechabites and the Order of the Good Samaritan) had strong support from antiformal evangelicals. The Washington Temperance Society was created in 1840 when six "moderate" drinkers realized they were not as "moderate" as they claimed to be. To solve the problem each pledged to abstain from all intoxicating liquor, and together they formed a new society which would free them from the tyranny of alcohol just as Washington had freed the nation from the tyranny of Britain. Like the American Temperance Union, the Washington Society used a teetotal pledge. But it was markedly different in that it stressed self-improvement rather than political action. Made up of many middle- and lower-class citizens (including many recovering alcoholics), the Washingtonians argued that heavy drinking interfered with employee job performance, thus alcohol kept workers from climbing the new industrial and commercial economic ladder. The only solution, the Washingtonians maintained, was to voluntarily abstain from the vice that frustrated personal success. The society provided social support for its members through entertaining cold-water banquets, musical performances, and Fourth of July picnics where orators fulminated against "King Alcohol."

Methodist and Baptist men and women (as well as those who had no religious affiliation) comprised the core of the movement. Perhaps the greatest reason Methodists and Baptists felt at home in the Washingtonian movement was that the organization's experience meetings were very similar to revival meetings. The Washingtonians had a dozen or more

reformed drinkers relate personal accounts of their lives
before and after they took the teetotal pledge. When emotions were at a fever pitch, drinkers were invited forward to
sign the pledge. Sometimes, as in New York in 1841,
hardened alcoholics and casual drinkers spontaneously left
their seats and streamed to the front of the auditorium even
before asked to do so.

The process of becoming a Washingtonian was very
similar to religious conversion. Like evangelicals seeking
God's forgiveness, those who became Washingtonians went
through a five-stage conversion process. First, drinkers were
"convicted" of the harm they were doing to their families,
their careers, and their own bodies. Second, they "struggled"
with the problem. Some bargained with themselves and
promised to "moderate" their drinking. Some even signed
the old pledge which demanded abstinence from spirits but
allowed the consumption of beer and wine. Third, when the
drinker realized that his current way of life could kill him,
he "converted" by coming forward, signing the Washingtonian pledge, and allowing his drinking habits to die.
Fourth, after taking the pledge, the new member "recognized" his new identity, that of a Washingtonian teetotaler.
Fifth, the convert was "reintegrated" into a new, nondrink-
ing community which encouraged him to keep the pledge
and provided entertainment, a support network, and, if
necessary, housing and a job.

Antiformal women played a significant role in the Washingtonian movement because antiformalist restrictions
against public female participation were not as rigid as those
of the formalists. Female exhorters and testifiers were central to the antiformal revivalist tradition, which paved the
way for greater influence in the temperance movement.
Women spoke at male Washingtonian meetings and kept the

organization afloat when masculine enthusiasm flagged. More important, they organized Martha Washington societies and published the first two female-edited temperance newspapers, the *New York Olive Plant* and the *New York Pearl*. They also created "a circle of sisters" which cut across class boundaries and distributed food and clothing to the temperate poor.

The vast majority of Southern blacks were untouched by the antialcohol crusade. Because African Americans were generally not allowed to gather in large unsupervised groups, Southern blacks rarely organized their own temperance societies. More important, available data suggests that black evangelicals were far less likely to become intoxicated than their white counterparts.

In the North, African Americans organized their first temperance chapter in 1829 when they formed the New Haven Temperance Society of the People of Color. By 1833 blacks created additional societies in Brooklyn, Baltimore, Boston, Hartford, and Middletown, Connecticut. After 1836, when blacks organized the New England Colored Temperance Society, black temperance advocates increasingly viewed the war on liquor and the war on slavery as being intrinsically the same. Frederick Douglass proclaimed, "I am a temperance man because I am an anti-slavery man." African Americans equated the two evils because they believed slave owners promoted drinking among slaves to keep them passive. Not only was alcohol seen as an ally of Southern slavery, it was condemned because it weakened the Northern black community by wasting money that could better be used to educate young people, build churches, or create vocational schools.

As with whites, temperance among blacks was a women's issue. When antiliquor societies were organized in Boston in

1833 the women's auxiliary had twice the number of members as the men's organization. Black female Pennsylvanians formed fourteen chapters of the Daughters of Temperance with fifteen hundred members. Black women also used personal moral influence and their presence within evangelical churches to encourage African American abstinence.

During the 1840s black temperance societies, with the help of black evangelical churches and clergymen, were extraordinarily successful in driving alcohol out of the Northern black community. African American churches disciplined those who violated congregational temperance edicts. Unlike whites, who had many other social groups to join if excommunicated, black evangelicals were more likely to submit to congregational demands since exclusion from the church was tantamount to ostracism from the center of social and community life. By the end of the decade the black temperance movement was so successful that only those who were at the very bottom of African American society had escaped the teetotal pledge. By the 1850s, having vanquished the demon of alcohol, Northern African Americans turned their attention away from temperance and focused exclusively on exorcising the demon of slavery.

Antislavery agitation grew powerful enough to convulse the Union partly because African American evangelicals joined forces with a significant number of white formal evangelicals to wage war on slaveholders, the majority of whom were white antiformalists. African American believers wanted to break the yoke of slavery, believing that God would again act in history to redeem his chosen people. Formal evangelicals played a leading role in the abolitionist movement and convinced others from their region (including many Northern antiformalists) that slavery was evil, that its westward expansion had to be stopped, and that white liberties were in danger if the slave power conspiracy was not destroyed. From the perspective of growing numbers of Congregationalists and Presbyterians, slavery violated the national covenant; God would punish the United States if slavery was not removed.

The formation of the American Colonization Society marks the beginning of the antebellum antislavery controversy. The Society was organized in 1816 and offered a "rational" solution to the problem of slavery. By ridding the nation of all emancipated African Americans, the ACS hoped to overcome the chief objection planters had to freeing their slaves, namely their fear of a large local free black population. Colonizationists encouraged owners voluntarily to emancipate their slaves, whereupon the Society would relocate the freed bondservants in Liberia. Under the ACS plan, slavery would be abolished gradually, and African Americans would return to their homeland to preach the Christian gospel to the African people. The ACS, one of many evangelical benevolent societies, was endorsed by most major Protestant denominations by 1830.

Free blacks viewed the American Colonization Society as an attempt to forcibly expel free blacks from the United States. Instead African Americans argued for ending Southern slavery and Northern racial discrimination as soon as possible. Richard Allen, founder of the African Methodist Episcopal church, wrote, "I have no doubt that there are many good men who do not see as I do; and who are for sending us to Liberia, but...they are not men of colour. This land, which we have watered with our tears and our blood, is now our mother country; and we are well satisfied to stay where wisdom abounds and the Gospel is free." Throughout the 1820s black opposition to colonization coalesced as local societies urging the immediate abolition of slavery were formed. By 1830 African Americans had organized at least fifty local abolitionist societies and in September of that year convened the First National Negro Convention to promote African American liberties.

Between 1830 and 1860 black organizers focused on three goals. First, they sought to improve the lives of Northern African Americans by promoting self-help and fighting for racial equality. Second, they cooperated with white abolitionists when possible and worked to raise the racial consciousness of white America. Third, they sponsored direct action, focusing on political action in the 1840s with some advocating violence to end slavery in the 1850s. Black evangelicals played crucial roles in each of these strategies. African American churches were central to improving life within Northern black communities. Black churches served as schools, social centers, relief agencies, and political meeting halls. As the black abolitionist Martin Delaney put it, "The Church is the Alpha and Omega of all things." Evangelicals were at the forefront of resisting racial discrimination in public services. Presbyterian Henry Highland Garnet forced the Utica and Schenectady Railroad to end its policy of segregated seating in the 1840s. In 1854 Elizabeth Jennings, an organist in a New York City Congregational church, successfully sued the Third Avenue line after she had been thrown out of a "whites-only" streetcar.

Beginning in the 1830s African American evangelicals worked closely with white abolitionists to raise public awareness of the evils of slavery. From 1831 to 1834 African Americans comprised one-half to three-fourths of the subscribers to William Lloyd Garrison's abolitionist newspaper, *The Liberator.* Many prominent black evangelicals—both men and women—joined Garrison on antislavery platforms.

In the 1840s and 1850s many black evangelicals expanded their approach by emphasizing direct action. The major focus was on political action. Beginning in the 1830s the Negro Convention movement worked to end restrictions (found in most Northern states) that either limited the number of black men who could vote or prohibited black suffrage altogether. Although efforts to reverse voting discrimination were generally unsuccessful, black evangelicals were still determined to use politics to attack slavery. Black evangelical leaders urged support for first the Liberty party and then the Free Soil party. In the 1850s, when the Republican party became the most powerful antislavery instrument, the vast majority of black voters rallied to the Republican banner.

Direct action meant more than casting ballots for freedom; it also included boycotts and civil disobedience. Beginning in the late eighteenth century many white Quakers resolved not to buy food produced by slave labor. In the 1830s this movement, known as the free produce movement, was adopted by a number of Northern black communities. Boycotts paled in significance when compared with civil disobedience. Harriet Tubman (AMEZ), a pious woman frequently guided by dreams and prayers, made nineteen trips into the South and led more than three hundred slaves to freedom. Tubman, who was called "Moses" for her prominent role in the Underground Railroad, never lost a single "passenger" to slaveholders and so frustrated the Southern aristocracy that a reward of $40,000 was established for her capture. Further north, black evangelicals frequently assisted runaway slaves by using church sanctuaries and parsonages to hide fugitives from authorities. Cincinnati's Zion Baptist Church, for example, protected as many as fourteen fugitives at a time.

From the beginning of the abolitionist movement, some black evangelicals believed violence would be necessary to bring the peculiar institution to its knees. Armed with Old Testament examples of divinely sanctioned destruction and New Testament apocalyptic hope, religious blacks were more open to violent solutions than were their white counterparts. The 1829 *Appeal* by Methodist David Walker advocated armed resistance, as a last resort, to destroy slavery. In promoting slave revolt Walker noted that "one good black man can put to death six white men." Fourteen years later Henry Highland Garnet made similar arguments in his *Address to the Slaves of the United States,* urging slaves to massive revolt: "Brethren, arise, arise! Strike for your lives and liberties. Now is the day and the hour. Let every slave throughout the land do this, and the days of slavery are numbered.... Rather die freemen than live to be slaves. Remember that you are FOUR MILLIONS."

Only a small minority of black evangelicals advocated physical resistance until the Fugitive Slave Law was passed in 1850. This new piece of legislation put all Northern African Americans at great risk because it brought those accused of being runaway slaves before special courts. Even blacks born in the North could be arraigned, as planters were free to charge anyone with dark skin with being an escaped slave. Jermain Loguen, a runaway slave, ridiculed Garrison's ideas of nonresistance; black Congregationalist Samuel Ringgold Ward called on blacks to use their "natural and inalienable rights of self-defence-self-protection." After the Supreme Court's Dred Scott decision of 1857, which denied the citizenship of free blacks and permitted the spread of slavery into the western territories, many other black evangelicals concluded that the peculiar institution could be destroyed only through violent means.

The black community's resistance to colonization steered many white humanitarians away from colonization and toward abolition. White activist Lewis Tappan related that black resistance to colonization "first induced Garrison and others to oppose it." In 1831 a number of white abolitionists—including Garrison, evangelicals Arthur Tappan and S. S. Jocelyn, and Quaker Benjamin Lundy—attended the First Annual Convention of People of Color as guests to discuss plans for creating a new national society dedicated to immediate emancipation.

In 1833 sixty-two abolitionists met in Philadelphia to create the American Anti-Slavery Society. In the new organization's Declaration of Sentiments the membership committed itself to immediate emancipation, total racial equality, and nonviolence. The declaration also condemned the compensation of slaveowners for their emancipated slaves and colonizationist plans to repatriate blacks in Africa. The founders of the antislavery organization came primarily from the center of American society. Many were white male evangelicals from Presbyterian and Congregational churches. Nonevangelical participants were also safely situated in positions of status, wealth, and influence: twenty-one were Quakers (including the poet John Greenleaf Whittier), and several more were Unitarians. Only four women (all Quakers) and three African Americans were among the sixty-two charter members.

Of the various groups in the American Anti-Slavery Society, none was more crucial than the formal evangelicals. Formal evangelicalism provided the strategy, organization, and energy that propelled abolitionism from the founding of the AASS to the Civil War.

Abolitionism's early strategy can be summed up in two words: "moral suasion." Members of the American

Anti-Slavery Society were convinced that when indifferent Northerners, misguided colonizationists, and slaveholding Southerners were presented with "the truth," they would turn from their wicked ways and embrace immediate emancipation. In promoting moral suasion, abolitionists used techniques that were working successfully in the contemporary revival and temperance campaigns. Well-advertised meetings were held in local churches where professional antislavery speakers (much like traveling evangelists and temperance lecturers) addressed the gathered citizenry. The guest speaker denounced the evils of slavery by relating emotionally laden anecdotes, using Scripture and common sense to show how bondage violated the laws of God and man, and urging his listeners to commit themselves to immediate emancipation. This strategy worked well in the North where the audience seldom needed to repent of more than supporting colonization.

Preaching abolition had no chance of success in the South. Southern whites were alarmed by Walker's *Appeal,* Garrison's *Liberator,* and Nat Turner's unsuccessful Virginia slave revolt, and they refused to allow antislavery men to spread their message. But abolitionists were not discouraged. They hoped that through proper organization and the use of modern transportation and communications, they might yet convert the heathen South to the antislavery gospel. If Northerners bore witness to the emancipationist message by joining abolitionist societies and signing petitions, if Northern churches professed opposition to slavery, if funds were raised to mass produce antislavery literature, and if the nation was blanketed with such newspapers, tracts, and books, then the South would hear the abolitionist message and hopefully repent of the sin of slavery. The American Anti-Slavery Society put the above plan into action using all the formal evangelical tactics perfected in two decades of organized benevolence. Like the temperance agents and missionaries before them, antislavery organizers spread across the North seeking to form local societies in every town, village, and hamlet. By 1838 the AASS announced it had 1,300 auxiliaries with a membership of 250,000, and had sent petitions with more than 400,000 signatures to Congress. Women played a major role in the drive as they created separate antislavery auxiliaries and were the majority of the petition signers. Between 1835 and 1837 the American Anti-Slavery Society sent more than a million pieces of literature to communities throughout the nation "to sow the good seed of abolition thoroughly over the whole country" in an effort known as "the great postal campaign." Having great faith in the written word, abolitionist leaders believed that once Southern officials, newspaper editors, and clergymen were confronted with their sin, they would abandon the peculiar institution.

The American Anti-Slavery Society hoped that the great postal campaign would put the country on a path to national redemption; instead, blanketing the nation with literature only revealed the weakness of moral suasion. Abolitionists realized that "the truth" did more than convert, it also antagonized. In the North antiabolitionists rioted, disrupted meetings, destroyed buildings, smashed printing presses, and murdered abolitionist editor Elijah Lovejoy at Alton, Illinois. In the South local elites, fearful that literate slaves would read abolitionist tracts and be inspired to revolt, broke into post offices and confiscated "incendiary literature" before it could be distributed. Northern and Southern foes of emancipation collaborated in the U.S. House of Representatives by enacting a "gag rule" that automatically tabled the discussion of petitions addressing slavery.

Southern antiformalists believed that all abolitionists, even those professing evangelical ideals, violated essential Christian principles. First, white Southerners argued that abolitionists refused to accept the authority of Scripture. A literal reading of the Bible revealed that the ancient Israelites owned slaves, that Jesus never spoke against slavery, and that Paul ordered servants to obey their masters and runaways to return to their owners. As a South Carolina Presbyterian put it, "If the Scriptures do not justify slavery, I know not what they justify." Second, emancipationists turned the church away from saving souls, its primary responsibility, toward "improving" society. Such actions created disharmony among believers by causing church members to fight over slavery. And by raising slaveholder fears, abolitionists made it harder for Southern churches to implement plantation missions. As a result, many slaves never heard the gospel message and were damned for eternity. Third, abolitionists disparaged the church's ability to encourage just and holy lives. Slavery, like any social institution, could be misused. But by using forceful instruction and strict discipline, local congregations could ensure that household heads did not abuse the women, children, and slaves under their authority. In short, antiformalists argued, the key was not to eliminate slavery but to turn slaveowners into Christian gentlemen.

Instead of sowing the seeds of repentance, moral suasion reaped a harvest of proslavery arguments and vociferous, sometimes violent, reactions. The American Anti-Slavery Society was in a quandary. Should it continue trying to persuade slaveholders to release their chattel, or should it try new approaches in the crusade against the peculiar institution?

The Garrisonian wing of the Society sought to stay the course of moral suasion and perfectionism. Believing that

even voting was a form of coercion and therefore "evil,"
Garrison and his supporters had no other option than to rely
on persuasion. This faction had become very impatient with
evangelicals within the Society, believing them to be not
entirely pure in belief and behavior. Garrisonians condemned evangelicals for not pushing hard enough to expel
slaveholders from the churches and for refusing to withdraw
from denominations that allowed slaveowners to receive
Communion. In addition, evangelicals were criticized for
placing their "sects" above the movement and for reverenc-
ing the Bible after it had been used by Southerners to justify
slavery. Finally, Garrisonians castigated the evangelicals for
not promoting total equality between the sexes and for not
opposing legalized American violence ranging from suffrage
to war.

Formal evangelicals had equally unkind things to say
about the Garrisonians. To oppose all antislavery methods
other than moral suasion was closed-minded and rigid. The
evangelicals also believed that attacking the Bible only
alienated the public and made the AASS appear to be a
band of infidels. Furthermore, promoting women to leadership positions and allowing them to speak before mixed or
"promiscuous" assemblies offended many formalists who
thought women should never leave their designated sphere.
Finally, most formalists still were Calvinist enough to believe
that human depravity required governments to maintain
order. Political action was not evil but necessary. Thus many
formal evangelicals wanted a pure antislavery political party
that, unlike the Whigs and Democrats, contained no slaveholders to corrupt its principles.

In 1840 the Garrisonian and evangelical wings of the
American Anti-Slavery Society broke into two separate organizations. Garrison controlled the 1840 convention, and

his group retained the original title. Considering Garrison's antidenominational and antibiblical convictions, it is not surprising to discover that 65 percent of the AASS leadership after 1840 was nonevangelical. The remaining third was divided evenly between formal and antiformal evangelicals. The anti-Garrisonian faction, led by Lewis Tappan, left to form the American and Foreign Anti-Slavery Society. The leaders of the new organization were nearly all evangelical, and two-thirds were formalists. The evangelical wing of the abolitionist movement broadened its strategy after 1840. While it continued to use literature and lectures to turn the Northern public against slavery, it also launched into politics and generally supported the new antislavery Liberty party. James Birney, New School Presbyterian and a leader of the AFASS, was the party's presidential nominee in both 1840 and 1844.

Evangelical abolitionists, now freed from the embarrassment of being linked to the "infidel" Garrisonians, renewed their efforts to get evangelical denominations to purge themselves of slaveholders. Persuading the evangelical denominations to strengthen their opposition to slavery was a formidable task. Emancipationists could refer to the early antislavery pronouncements of a number of evangelical bodies. John Wesley condemned slavery as a "villainy" that violated "all the laws of Justice, Mercy, and Truth." After the American Revolution, Methodists promised to exclude all members who did not free their slaves within two years. In 1789 Baptists argued that human bondage was "a violent deprivation of the rights of nature and inconsistent with a republican government." In 1818 the Presbyterian General Assembly pronounced "the voluntary enslaving of one part of the human race by another [to be] a gross violation of the most precious and sacred rights of human nature [and] utterly inconsistent with the law of God." The problem was that evangelical denominations were far more tolerant of slavery in particular cases than they were of slavery in the abstract. Numerous complications clouded the issue at the local level, making specific judgments difficult. Members often received slaves through marriage and inheritance. In the Deep South state laws forbade manumission. Many members believed that freeing elderly slaves too old to work at wage labor was more objectionable than retaining them as slaves. Because of the confusion arising from specific cases, evangelical churches gradually compromised, and by the 1830s evangelicals throughout the South owned bondservants. Abolitionists found that after slavery had grown surreptitiously for decades, uprooting it from existing denominations would be an enormous task.

White formalist and antiformalist denominations had five factions battling to define each religious body's position regarding slavery. The *comeouters* were the most vociferous opponents to slavery. They wanted their home congregations, their regional organizations, and their national denominational agencies to condemn slavery unequivocally and break all ties with any religious bodies condoning slaveholding. Should the churches fail to accept their demands, the comeouters—quoting the Book of Revelation, "Come out of her, my people, that ye be not partakers of her sins, and that ye receive not of her plagues"—were willing to abandon their old denominations and create new antislavery churches. If churches would not purify themselves by condemning slavery, at least the comeouters could maintain their own purity by forsaking the churches.

Three centrist factions considered denominational loyalty more important than taking an ideologically pure position on slavery. *Denominational abolitionists* agreed with the comeouters' critique of evangelical religion. But they were not discouraged by initial failures to redeem the churches and continued the fight to expel all slaveholders from evangelical congregations. They also worked to push denominational mission, education, and publishing boards in an antislavery direction. *Moderate antislavery advocates* considered slavery evil but believed the automatic excommunication of slaveholders, with no regard for extenuating circumstances, to be extreme. While the moderates supported the establishment of antislavery denominational agencies, they also believed that moral suasion would fail if slaveholders were forced out of churches that preached an antislavery message. *Conservatives* considered slavery to be a political issue that should not be discussed within the churches. Distinguishing between "the things that are God's" and "the things which are Caesar's," conservatives believed that state legislatures should rule on slavery and that churches should restrict themselves to purely religious matters. Politically, conservative evangelicals gravitated toward gradual, voluntary emancipation and considered colonization to be "the only practical and peaceful solution."

Seceders held views opposite from the comeouters, but their solution—breaking denominational ties—was the same as the most radical antislavery advocates. The seceders believed that abolitionists poisoned the churches and that antislavery societies were another assault on local congregational self-determination. They did not seek gradual emancipation or political neutrality but were vigorous proslavery partisans. They believed that the Bible sanctioned slaveholding and that the duty of the church was to "Christianize" slavery by disciplining uncharitable owners and evangelizing bondservants. The seceders wanted to force the major denominations to agree that slave ownership was no barrier to membership or to positions of leadership. Should a religious body fail officially to condone slaveholding, the seceders preferred to leave rather than contaminate themselves by fellowshiping with those who put political passion above the authority of Scripture.

Between 1840 and 1860 these five groups battled for control of the major evangelical denominations. Some religious bodies experienced only minor skirmishes. Congregationalism had no Southern wing, so there were virtually no conservatives and seceders trying to curtail antislavery discussion. But denominational abolitionists and antislavery moderates debated whether it was proper to contribute money to benevolent agencies that had not severed all connections to slavery. By contrast the Disciples of Christ had no significant Northern wing pushing them toward abolition, and therefore had no seceders seeking to silence antislavery sentiment. Instead the Disciples were dominated by conservatives like Alexander Campbell who argued that Scripture did not condemn slavery, that disciplining members for owning slaves was unbiblical, and that compensated emancipation and colonization were the best political solutions to the slavery issue.

The battle over antislavery policy was the most fierce in three denominations. The Presbyterians went through schisms in 1837 and 1857. The first denominational split occurred in response to New School and Old School disagreements over theology, seminaries, and cooperation with the Congregationalists. In addition, Southern presbyteries distrusted growing antislavery sentiment within the New School faction. In 1837 the Old School, which gravitated toward old-fashioned Calvinism and was skeptical of the benevolent empire, drove the New School from the denomination. The New School, faced with no other alternative, then created its own Presbyterian assembly. After the schism the Old School conservatives pacified their dominant Southern wing by pronouncing slavery to be a political issue unrelated to the mission of the church. But antislavery controversy continued within the New School as abolitionist members, believing the New School to be "a church that maintains fraternal fellowship with robbers," pushed for the exclusion of all slaveholders. Denominational abolitionists had little success, and in frustration some "came out" and formed abolitionist Presbyterian congregations. Together the comeouters, the Free Presbyterians, and various Scottish Presbyterian sects—one-sixth of all Presbyterians—vigorously condemned slavery between 1837 and the Civil War. Meanwhile, centrists (antislavery moderates and conservatives) kept the New School from tilting in either an abolitionist or proslavery direction. The New School fence-straddling kept the Northern and Southern wings together until 1857, when about one-tenth of the New School seceded to form their own Southern Presbyterian denomination.

Baptists were also divided over the slavery issue. Because Baptists had an antiformal tradition that stressed individual conscience and congregational autonomy, and because they had a powerful Southern wing, Baptist seceders were far more powerful than were their Presbyterian equivalents. In 1845 more than half the Baptists formed a separate Southern Baptist Convention after the denomination's foreign mission board announced it would not sponsor slaveholding missionaries. One might expect that once the Southerners had left, the Northern remnant would have taken an uncompromising antislavery position. This was not the case, however, as centrists kept the Northern Baptists from moving beyond general statements that slavery was evil. For instance, conservative Francis Wayland, the president of Brown University, ensured that the American Baptist Missionary Union was "purely for missions" and "equally free from slavery and antislavery." Northern Baptists, having a strong antiformal tradition which separated church and state, were particularly susceptible to conservative arguments that slavery was a political question which ought not concern the church. Most Northern associations agreed that slavery was morally wrong but, fearing dissension, they avoided specific political recommendations and resolutions declaring all slaveholders to be non-Christian. Baptist abolitionists were angry over their inability to get their coreligionists to adopt an active antislavery position. By 1850 thousands of Baptist comeouters, along with an even larger group of Freewill Baptists, presented an uncompromised witness against slavery.

Nor did Methodists escape division. The followers of John Wesley had a tradition of opposing slavery through preaching, exhortation, and discipline rather than through political action. As a result, abolitionist appeals to drive all slaveholders from the churches struck many Methodists as being unnecessary, uncharitable, and counterproductive. Peter Cartwright stated, "I was opposed to slavery, though I did not meddle with it politically, yet I felt it my duty to bear my testimony against the moral wrong of slavery." Cartwright's solution was apolitical and typically Methodist: "If the religion of Jesus Christ will not finally bring about emancipation of the slaves, nothing else will." As with other issues, antiformalist Methodists believed that spiritual, not organizational, solutions provided the answer to society's problems, and that slavery's demise depended on redeeming sinners one by one.

The centrist position of most Methodists frustrated the abolitionist faction. Methodist abolitionists were angry that the majority did not wish to cleanse the denomination from the sin of slaveholding. About 2 percent of all Methodists "came out" and created abolitionist Wesleyan Methodist congregations. By contrast Southern Methodists thought Northerners were too stringent regarding slaveholding. Southern Methodists seceded from the national body (taking 43 percent of all Methodists with them) in 1844 shortly after the Methodist General Conference suspended James Andrew, a Georgia bishop who had not released his slaves. Even after the Southern wing had departed, Northern Methodists were slow to take a firm stand on slavery. It was not until after the Fugitive Slave Law infuriated numerous Northerners that the General Assembly began to support political action against slavery.

White evangelical churches were thus far from being abolitionist bodies. The Presbyterians were dominated by centrists, and the Baptists and Methodists had enormous numbers of proslavery members. The reaction of each denomination to the slavery issue was consistent with its formalist or antiformalist tradition. The relatively large proportion of Presbyterians who were "comeouters" or who joined antislavery sects reflected that denomination's formalist organizational emphasis, allegiance to institutional benevolence, and commitment to upholding the national covenant. By contrast, seceders greatly outnumbered comeouters and antislavery sectarians among antiformalist Baptists and Methodists. This result is not surprising given the Baptist and Methodist emphasis on lay authority and local control, their commitment to redeeming sinners over changing society, and their suspicion of interdenominational efforts at reform. As with Sabbatarianism and temperance, formalists gravitated toward organized national efforts to root out evil, whereas antiformalists generally endorsed personal and/or denominational solutions to wrongdoing.

As with other aspects of evangelical belief and behavior, the struggle to redeem America spilled over into secular aspects of national life. With 60 percent of the United States population under the direct influence of evangelical Protestantism, formalist-antiformalist disputes paralleled and reinforced differences between major political parties.

From the mid-1830s until 1852 American politics was dominated by Whigs and Democrats. The Whigs frequently were members of the emerging American commercial order, were "inner-directed," and supported efforts to promote self-control in others as well as themselves. Being comfortable with large impersonal organizations, the Whigs advocated an "American System" wherein government used the Bank of the United States, the protective tariff, and state-financed internal improvements to promote economic growth. The Whigs also supported innovations such as paper money and incorporation laws to promote business. Although they were strong believers in the family (where the values of inner-direction and self-control were taught), Whigs believed schools and prohibition were needed to discipline the general population, and government-supported poorhouses, insane asylums, juvenile reformatories, and penitentiaries were needed to impart internal order and self-discipline to those who had not learned self-control from other sources. In general the Whigs sought to add structure to an American society they believed was suffering from a lack of order.

By contrast, Democrats attracted the more economically marginal, urban laborers and Southern or Western farmers, who were uncomfortable with the rate and direction of economic change. Democrats saw themselves as "outsiders," were "tradition-directed," and sought freedom from new "monster" institutions imposed on them by the economic elite. Unlike the Whigs, Jacksonian Democrats saw the American System as a series of "British devices to enslave a people," and viewed bank loans, paper money, and business incorporation as diabolical inventions designed to entrap ordinary farmers and laborers. They distrusted many social innovations. Democrats were more suspicious of public education than were the Whigs, and Catholic partisans established their own parochial school system. From the Democratic perspective, prohibition laws and state-supported asylums did not teach self-control to social deviants so much as restrict the liberties of the less powerful. Democrats also feared the well-organized formalist benevolent empire and opposed any "union of church and state." Overall Democrats favored the traditional institutions of family, local church, and small communities, believing that large impersonal institutions imposed too much order on ordinary Americans, thus taking away their freedom.

The Whig-Democrat dichotomy thus paralleled that of formalists and antiformalists. Just as Whigs sought to create economic order through the protective tariff and the U.S. Bank, formalists sought to create moral order through national missionary, Sunday School, Bible, and tract societies. Just as Democrats sought to keep political authority in the hands of state and local authorities, antiformalists favored benevolence only when conducted by denominational agencies and relied on local church discipline to form Christian character. Whigs and formalists believed the prohibition of alcohol was desirable, whereas Democrats and antiformalists generally thought drinking to be a matter of private choice. Not surprisingly, during the 1830s and early 1840s Congregationalists and Presbyterians were overwhelmingly Whigs, and Methodists were most often Democrats. Baptists were somewhat more Whiggish than Methodists but, when viewed nationally, Baptists also tilted toward the party of Jackson.

Social forces and political events disrupted this political-religious alignment in the late 1840s and 1850s. Northern Methodists and Baptists had become more affluent, assumed more political and social power, and increasingly saw themselves as part of the nation's dominant culture. As a result, Northern antiformalist worship became less emotional, their ministers were better educated and presented more sophisticated sermons, and church activities were more organized and businesslike. Northern Baptists and Methodists began to see themselves as modernizers who were very different from their planter coreligionists in the traditionalist South. In addition, Baptists and Methodists cooperated with formal evangelicals in the battle to control and reform waves of Catholics entering the country in the 1840s and 1850s. When Northern antiformalists were the targets of Sabbatarian, education, and prohibition laws, they were outraged; but when formalists targeted "unassimilable" Catholic immigrants, many Northern antiformalists agreed that legislative action was necessary to preserve American morality. In the face of Southern slavery and Catholic immigration, Northern antiformalists found they had more in common with their former religious adversaries than they did with their fellow Democrats. Meanwhile, Southern Presbyterians, who once looked down on rustic Baptists and Methodists, were alienated by Northern attacks on Southern culture and religion. Once Southern Presbyterians had joined Southern Baptists and Southern Methodists in seceding from their national bodies, they felt even more kinship with their former adversaries and joined them in defending "the Southern way of life."

In 1854 the Republican party replaced the Whigs on the American political landscape. Over the next six years the new organization gathered support from a number of sources. Republicans wanted government actively to promote economic growth through state-supported land grant univer-

sities, a transcontinental railroad, centralized banking, a
moderately high tariff, homesteading, paper currency, and
other economic initiatives which attracted many ex-Whigs.
They also added Know-Nothing partisans by joining in
nativist hysteria, promoting prohibition, and offering man-
datory public education as a way to civilize and Americanize
recently arrived Catholics. Republicans also absorbed many
Liberty party supporters and Free Soil Democrats by opposing the extension of slavery into the western territories. By
combining these groups, the Republicans became the dominant party in the North. Yet the new party was virtually
nonexistent in the South. Unlike the Republicans, who had
become a sectional party, the Democrats still had support
throughout the nation in the 1850s. But with Free Soil
Democrats leaving and ex-Southern Whigs joining, the Democratic party was increasingly influenced by its Southern wing.
After the Dred Scott decision Southern Democrats asked for
more protection of slavery than what Northern Democrats
were willing to grant. In 1860 the Southern Democrats, like
the Southern Methodists, Baptists, and New School Presbyterians before them, severed relations with their Northern brethren.

The emergence of the Republican party not only hastened
a rupture in the Union, it also produced new denominational alignments that would last long after the Civil War.
The majority of Northern Methodists, Baptists, and Disciples joined forces with their old formalist opponents in
support of the Republicans. Common fears of Catholics and
slavery had overwhelmed old concerns over class. Meanwhile, Southern Presbyterians, horrified by Republican plans
to contain slavery geographically, joined Southern antiformalists and supported the Democratic party. This new political
alignment, shaped in part by shifting coalitions of formalists
and antiformalists, lasted long after the Civil War.

5

The Coming of the Lord

THE DIVISION between formal and antiformal evangelicals involved not simply differences over behavior in this world but over the nature of the world to come. From the start, Christians wrestled with the meaning of Christ's prophecy that in end times (which he suggested were very near), "all the tribes of the earth ... shall see the Son of man coming in the clouds of heaven with power and great glory." Eschatology, or the study of the last things, intensified with the Protestant Reformation. Despite the efforts of Martin Luther and John Calvin, who followed Augustine in interpreting the millennium allegorically, many Protestants believed in a literal millennium that would last exactly one thousand years. From the literalist point of view, every seal, vial, trumpet, dragon, and beast mentioned in the prophetic books referred to a past, present, or future person or historical event. By correctly matching biblical images to history, and by interpreting prophetic "days" as years, scholars believed they could predict the return of Jesus and the beginning of the millennium. For these thinkers, history and prophecy were two sides of the same coin: history was what God had done, prophecy was what biblical writers predicted God would yet do.

During the 1790s American millennialists divided into

two distinct schools of thought. Postmillennialists (also called millennialists) believed that while Jesus' spirit would actively promote health, prosperity, and righteousness during the one thousand years, he would not visibly appear until after the millennium had concluded. Premillennialists (also called millenarians) disagreed, contending that Christ's visible return would occur *before* the millennium and that Jesus would be physically present during the saints' thousand-year reign. Generally, premillennialists were far more pessimistic than postmillennialists, since they believed that human history would descend into chaos, that the world would be struck with a series of natural cataclysms, and that the Messiah alone was capable of restoring order and instituting the millennium. Although few realized it at the time, premillennial sentiments were not only growing among white Baptists and Methodists, but similar thinking was emerging among African Americans as well. Slaves in particular gravitated toward premillennial views as they realized that the Day of Jubilee would come not from white spiritual progress but only by an Act of God. By 1820 formal, antiformal, and African American evangelicals all looked to the Coming of the Lord; but their social location influenced their thought regarding the timing of Jesus' return and what to expect when he arrived.

In this context formalist theologians revised and refined their eschatological theories. The vast majority of formalist clergy were postmillennialists who predicted steady progress toward the beginning of earthly paradise. Postmillennialism was strongest among New England's Congregational preachers but was also common among Presbyterian and evangelical Episcopalian ministers and English-speaking clergy of Calvinist-influenced Dutch and German Reformed churches. With such antebellum luminaries as Lyman Beecher, Horace Bushnell, and Charles Finney endorsing postmillennial views, the formalist laity embraced postmillennialism and organized to hasten the coming of God's Kingdom.

There are numerous reasons why formal evangelicals were attracted to postmillennialism. This brand of eschatology was endorsed by the best-trained theological minds of the nation. Postmillennialism was orderly—it postulated a gradual improvement in society before the thousand years rather than a disruptive cataclysmic event. Postmillennialism's gradual approach meant that Christians could either slow down or speed up progress toward the millennium, which appealed to formalists who were used to controlling social and political institutions. Overall, formalist postmillennialism reflected an optimistic, comfortable view of social and spiritual advancement.

Formal evangelicals believed that preaching, missions, and prayer would hasten the coming Kingdom. Preaching was absolutely vital. Spreading the Word through oral and written means promoted individual conversions which, according to evangelicals, laid the groundwork for social reform and resulted in improved character and higher intelligence. Because massive conversions were seen as precursors to the millennium, formalists promoted the American Home Missionary Society, the American Education Society (for the training of ministers), the American Sunday School Union, the American Tract Society, the American Bible Society, and many other evangelistic organizations.

Missionary endeavors went far beyond winning unchurched pioneers in the West. Because converting "heathens" and Jews allegedly hastened the millennium, formal evangelicals organized to convert these people as well. The American Board of Commissioners for Foreign Missions, the international counterpart of the AHMS, was dominated by

Presbyterians and Congregationalists. Although Baptists, Methodists, and Episcopalians had representatives working in distant corners of the globe, these denominations never had more than twenty missionaries operating at any one time. By comparison the ABCFM sponsored nearly a thousand foreign missionaries between 1810 and 1860. The ABCFM also sent its agents to native American peoples. Congregationalist missionaries, for example, were the first to bring the Christian gospel to the inhabitants of the Hawaiian Islands.

Postmillennialism, at least in its nineteenth-century manifestation, viewed the future optimistically. As a result, two traditional millennial portents, frequent earthquakes and wars, were downplayed if not altogether dismissed from formalist eschatology. To the educated inhabitants of America's comfortable class, earthquakes were not the result of supernatural intervention but were understandable geological events. Likewise, wars were not predestined but, with the proper reordering of social values, were avoidable. Postmillennialists were more likely to join peace societies than to consider conflict the result of God's judgment.

Even though formalists were activists prone to organizing, one remnant from the Calvinist past hampered their enthusiasm. Just as traditional Calvinism argued that each person's salvation was predestined, it also contended that the future (as prophesied in the Bible) had already been determined by the Almighty. If so, efforts to hasten the millennium were fruitless. In the 1830s Charles Finney altered orthodox teaching regarding the millennium, just as he radically modified Calvinist theology on salvation. The millennium, according to Finney, was similar to the Second Birth in that human choice could accelerate the arrival of each. The evangelist argued that the only thing that delayed the long-awaited Kingdom was human will. In 1835 Finney wrote, "If the church will do her duty the millennium may come in this country in three years."

Such prodding from formal evangelical ministers helped propel Northern formalists into the plethora of voluntary societies—such as the American Female Reform Society, the American Anti-Slavery Society, the American Temperance Society, the General Union for the Promotion of the Christian Sabbath, and the American Peace Society—aimed at purifying the nation so as to make America a holy instrument in the Lord's hands. Even the New York Maternal Association entered the crusade as the 1832 edition of *The Mother's Manual* announced that "mothers will have a conspicuous part to perform [in] the introduction of the *Millennium*. When every nursery shall become a little sanctuary, and not before, will the earth be filled with the knowledge and glory of the Lord."

By the 1840s Northern formalist leaders celebrated the progress made in redeeming the nation's collective soul by a host of benevolent and reform societies. "Allow me to say," the moderator of the New School Presbyterian General Assembly proclaimed to a London audience in 1846, "that, in America, the state of society is without parallel in universal history. With all our mixtures, there is a leaven of heaven; there is goodness there; there is excellent principle there. I really believe that God has got America within anchorage, and that upon that arena, He intends to display his prodigies for the millennium."

Southern formalists were equally optimistic about America's millennial role. They too believed society would gradually get better and better as the cosmic clock ticked toward the blessed thousand years. Southern Presbyterians believed that progress toward the millennium would be calm and steady and would involve no serious disruptions. This point of view suggested that slavery would be perfected, not destroyed, in the future age. During the millennium slaves would be converted, educated, and voluntarily work at whatever task they were given. Assuming such a benign system of human bondage in the future, one writer suggested that slavery "might have existed in Paradise and may continue through the Millennium." While no Southern formalist could guarantee slavery's continuance in the millennial age, they increasingly argued there was no reason why God could not let the peculiar institution continue once it had been cleansed of abuses.

At mid-century formal evangelicals saw only two major barriers to America assuming its millennial role. The first potential roadblock was Roman Catholic immigration. While Catholics had been in America ever since the colonial period, their presence had seldom created major alarm in the Protestant community. Catholics were few in number (only about 100,000 in 1815), shared a common ethnic heritage with the dominant social classes, and were often landed gentry. But Catholics who entered the United States after 1815 were numerous, non-British (usually Irish or German), and often desperately poor. By 1855 adherents to the Roman church had grown from an insignificant minority to the largest single denomination in the country, claiming a church population of four million souls.

For evangelicals, who learned from infancy that the pope was the Antichrist and that the Roman church was the Whore of Babylon, the Catholic influx was nothing less than catastrophic. Just as America was on the verge of leading the world into the millennium, the devil counterattacked by sending Catholic legions into America. Congregationalist Samuel F. B. Morse, inventor of the telegraph, warned against growing Catholic power: "The serpent has already commenced his coil about our limbs, and the lethargy of his poison is creeping over us."

Formal evangelicals (and a good number of antiformalists) believed that the best way to contain Catholicism was a combination of persuasion, economic coercion, and political action. Persuading Roman Catholics to convert to evangelical Protestantism was difficult because recent immigrants rarely attended Protestant churches. Written exposés, such as the *Awful Disclosures of Maria Monk*, which alleged immoral conduct among priests and nuns, alienated far more Catholics than they convinced. The only place where Protestants were guaranteed access to a Catholic audience was in the public school system. But when the Roman church countered with its own parochial school system, evangelical efforts to convert large numbers of Catholics to Protestant belief systems failed again. Economic coercion was directed primarily toward urban Irish Catholic laborers who often saw signs in store windows, "No Irish Need Apply." (German Catholics, who were more likely to become independent farmers or shopkeepers, were less susceptible.) Politics appeared to be the most effective arena for combating the growing Catholic population. In the mid-1850s the nativists organized the American, or Know-Nothing, party on an anti-Catholic, anti-immigration platform. Playing on Protestant fears, the Know-Nothings warned that Catholic influence would culminate in the American president bowing and kissing the pope's toes. Former Whigs, particularly in Northern urban centers, flocked toward the Know-Nothing party. But after the Republicans adopted anti-Catholicism, Northern ex-Whigs quickly moved to the Republican party.

Postmillennialists also believed that slavery could keep America from fulfilling its millennial role. By the 1850s

Northern formalists were generally convinced that God could not use the nation to initiate the millennium until slavery was purged from the land. From the Northern point of view, the Antichrist now appeared in the form of the slave-power conspiracy. At the same time Southern formalists were becoming increasingly convinced that a perpetual system of human slavery was part of the providential plan. To these postmillennialists the Antichrist was anyone who opposed their divine errand of expanding slaveholding territory. For both Northern and Southern formalists, slavery would determine America's role in promoting the millennium. But because their views on slavery were so different, the nation would have to experience severe tribulation before the millennial dreams of either camp could come true.

By late 1857 postmillennialists had reason to question whether the new order was as close as they had earlier supposed. Roman Catholics continued to migrate to American shores in huge numbers as Germans arrived at a pace that outstripped even the Irish. The slavery controversy increasingly divided the nation. And the United States was struggling to emerge from the Panic of 1857. Yet in the depths of national despair a remarkable religious revival renewed postmillennial hopes.

The Union Prayer Meeting Revival of 1858 grew out of formalist institutions. The Young Men's Christian Associations, the latest in a long series of formalist-led interdenominational agencies, were the revival's chief promoters. The Old School Presbyterians were prominent denominational sponsors of the awakening. Despite its formalist origins, the revival spread rapidly outward from the Northeastern cities where it originated to influence all geographic regions and white social classes. Some contemporaries calculated that a half-million people were converted in the span of twelve months. One traveler observed, "From Omaha City, Nebraska, to Washington, *there was a line of prayer-meetings along the whole length of the road;* so that, wherever a Christian traveller stopped to spend the evening, he could find a crowded prayer-meeting, across the entire breadth of our vast republic."

Much of the revival's attraction was its emphasis on unity. It was as though Americans looked at the economic, denominational, and sectional differences that were tearing the nation apart, realized they had no solutions for social divisiveness, and called on God to heal the nation's wounds. "Unity" was emphasized throughout the awakening. Organizers sought to overcome class differences by consciously including "everyone"—there were special meetings for women as well as businessmen, workingmen, policemen, firemen, and other occupational groups. Those who spoke at prayer meetings were not allowed to state their denominational affiliation, and "the advancement of sectarian views [was] not tolerated in any form." Hopes for unity soared as religious groups outside the evangelical fold, principally Unitarians, Universalists, Roman Catholics, and even a few Jews, had kind words for the prayer meeting revival. Slavery was not allowed to divide participants as no one was allowed to condemn slaveholding as a "sin," nor were prayer requests on behalf of fugitive slaves allowed. In one last desperate attempt, American evangelicals sought to pray the nation's problems away.

But prayers for millennial unity were not answered. Class, denominational, and sectional differences were still present after the year-long wave of religious euphoria had subsided. Ironically the Civil War, not the millennium, came on the heels of the heralded Union Prayer Meeting Revival.

*

Most antiformalists were postmillennialists who believed that God would use the United States to introduce the coming millennium. The postmillennial image of a world constantly growing better was consistent with everyday experiences of material progress and common ideas of self-betterment and personal independence. The distinctive beliefs of various denominations reinforced millennialist thinking. Methodists, whose Arminian theology emphasized free will, were comfortable with believing that human agency could make the world better, thus paving the way for "the spiritual reign of Christ." The Disciples of Christ, following the lead of Alexander Campbell, were generally in the postmillennial camp, as were Baptists. The *Christian Review* represented the views of the Baptist majority when it proposed "to show that the period (the millennium) predicted in the Bible, when the religion of Jesus shall have subverted all other systems, is at hand."

Even though antiformalists generally favored postmillennialism, a minority held premillennial views. In 1799 New England Baptist Abraham Cummings, reacting to the French Revolution and its American partisans, warned against trying to bring on the millennium through revolution, instead arguing that Christ would suddenly appear to judge the world. In the 1830s John Hersey, a Methodist circuit rider, contended that "a thousand years enjoyed on earth as a holy Sabbath" was imminent, but that this happy event would only occur *after* "Christ...come[s] again to dispel the gloomy clouds of sin; to elevate his church on earth, and to reign gloriously in Zion." Disciples preacher Arthur Crihfield discounted postmillennial claims of spiritual progress, noting that "the present amount of spiritual influence is not likely to produce a better state of society; that, it is probably that the coming of the Lord is nigh."

Premillennialism echoed many antiformalist ideas. Like antiformal evangelicals generally, millenarians saw themselves as social outsiders. Thus they looked forward to Christ's visible return, when the Son of God would reverse the existing order and "many that are first shall be last; and the last shall be first." As a rule, antiformalists participated only in voluntary, nonlegislative reform; premillennialists argued that human efforts to redeem society were doomed to fail and that believers should focus only on saving individual sinners. Unlike formalists, antiformalists were somewhat suspicious of innovations and technological change; likewise, premillennialists saw steamships and railroads not as harbingers of the millennium but as a "powerful stimulus to avarice, to worldliness, to selfishness in every form." Premillennialism, like antiformalism, placed great emphasis on commonsense interpretations of the Bible and stressed the literal interpretation of the Word so emphatically that Adventism was sometimes called "Bibleism." Of all of the antiformal groups, the hard-line Calvinists probably had most in common with premillennialists. They contended that God was all-powerful, that humans could do nothing to change their eternal fates, and that both salvation and history were predetermined by the Almighty.

With numerous similarities between antiformal and premillennial thought, the potential for a powerful antebellum millenarian movement was great. In fact, lower-class whites often believed in folk apocalyptic, an attitude expecting the world's imminent end which lacked an overarching theological structure. Like the few scholarly premillennialists, many ordinary people were convinced that God would soon bring existing governments to an end in a dramatic series of cataclysmic events. But most common folk did not try to gauge the end times by searching Scripture for clues; instead

they looked to the "signs of the end times" that were
generally ignored by postmillennialists.

Believers in folk apocalyptic watched political disputes
and unusual natural phenomena for these signs. They justi-
fied their omen-seeking on biblical passages such as Luke
21:25, where Jesus spoke of the last days: "And there shall be
signs in the sun, and in the moon, and in the stars; and upon
the earth distress of nations, with perplexity. . . ." While
"wars and rumors of wars" were among the signs of the end
times, ordinary folk paid the most attention to unusual
natural phenomena. Earthquakes were often seen as a warning to repent. When a series of earthquakes struck Kentucky, a local millenarian "expected immediate destruction,
had no hope of seeing the dawn of another day. Eternity, oh
Eternity was just at hand, and all of us unprepared. . . ."
Many watched the heavens for portents of the end. Some saw
impending disaster in the northern lights. In 1827 a New
Yorker said he had observed "the muskets, bayonets, and
knapsacks of the men [in the Lord's Army]" spread across
the northern skies. When the "front rank approached the
western horizon," the Forces of Good battled the Legions of
Satan. In 1831 a solar eclipse caused many to wonder if the
world's end was drawing near. When later the same year an
atmospheric disturbance known as the "Three Blue Days"
made the sun appear to change color from New York to
South Carolina, some Philadelphians saw in the unusual
spectacle "a sad augury of coming evil." Other sky-watchers
claimed to have seen the letters G-O-D emerge in the
heavens "from a long narrow (or serpentine) silvery colored
belt."

Unexplained natural disasters provided further "proof"
that folk anxieties about the world's end were well founded.
In 1816 abnormally cold weather disrupted the northeastern

United States as portions of New England had snow and ice for the entire year. While the unusual weather was caused by the eruptions of an Indonesian volcano, no one in the United States knew this to be true at the time. As a result, many claimed "the year without a summer" was a divine warning. Sixteen years later cholera struck New York and New England. Medical doctors were unable to understand or effectively treat the disease, and half of those infected died. In the absence of other explanations many turned to religion, seeking to appease Almighty God.

For ordinary Americans predisposed to seeing God's hand in earthquakes, the heavens, and in unexplained disaster, the world's imminent collapse was only a misfortune away. Folk apocalyptic, however, was only an attitude. Until someone forged a popular theology that gave the attitude an intellectual structure, hopes and fears regarding the Second Coming tended to dissipate once the immediate portent or crisis had passed. In the 1830s and early 1840s a "reluctant prophet" named William Miller provided Northeastern antiformalists a clearly understandable biblical explanation of how the Second Coming would occur in 1843 or 1844. In so doing Miller provided a premillennial intellectual construct which validated the fears of folk apocalyptic. When Miller focused antiformalist minds and emotions on the end times, he began America's first premillennial mass movement.

The Baptist farmer-preacher had spent much of his youth as a devotee of Thomas Jefferson, even to the point of identifying himself as a deist for a period of time. Miller was essentially self-taught (his boyhood home had only three books—the Bible, a hymnal, and a prayer book), and after his conversion in 1816 he decided to search Scripture for himself in order to discover its timeless truth. Miller believed if he studied the Bible scientifically he would be able to resolve all apparent contradictions, thus proving Scripture's divine authorship. The Vermont preacher was essentially a Common Sense literalist who believed that if people read the Word with the eyes of faith and the proper interpretive technique they would understand God's eternal message. Faith was crucial but so was method, so Miller created fourteen commonsense rules that would allow any seeker correctly to interpret Holy Writ. While the fourteen dictums emphasized a literal interpretation of the Bible, they also observed that some passages made no literal sense and had to be interpreted figuratively. But under Miller's system, all figurative passages had the same exact symbolic meaning— "beasts" meant "kingdoms," "mountains" meant "governments," "waters" meant "people," and "days" meant "years." By 1818 Miller had decoded all of Scripture and in the process discovered that the Second Coming was only twenty-five years away! In spite of the shocking revelation, Miller lacked the confidence to spread the good news. Only after he had received God's blessing in a dream did he dare to share his ideas privately among friends and relatives.

Miller's success in attracting a large following was chiefly due to the entrepreneurial Joshua Himes, a preacher within the Christian Connexion, a Northern version of the Disciples of Christ, whom Miller met in 1839. Himes quickly became Miller's chief manager, organizer, and promoter, utilizing all the publicity techniques available to antebellum evangelicals and inventing a few of his own. Almost immediately Himes had a printer issue a new edition of Miller's book on the Second Coming. By early 1840 the publicist founded a Boston newspaper, *Signs of the Times*, which was dedicated to propagating Miller's views. A second periodical, *The Midnight Cry*, began publication in New York City a few years later. Himes had agents traversing the Northern states

and selling subscriptions to the Millerite papers. The Adventists even published their own hymnal, *The Millennial Harp*.
Between 1840 and 1843 the Second Adventists distributed
four million pieces of literature; according to Adventist
records, 600,000 copies of *The Midnight Cry* were disseminated in the first five months of 1842. By 1844 there were as
many as fifty thousand hard-core Millerites. Up to a million
evangelicals believed Miller's predictions might possibly be
true.

Millerites were not content simply to use earlier media
techniques; they had two major innovations of their own.
The first was Himes's "Great Tent," a fifty-five-foot-high
canvas monstrosity capable of seating four thousand listeners. Not only did the Great Tent attract attention, it combined the best features of the camp meetings (which were
large but often plagued by rowdies and bad weather) and
protracted meetings (which were safely held inside churches
but were usually not big enough to draw crowds above
several hundred). With Himes's innovation Miller was the
first American evangelist who was guaranteed rural crowds
that were dry, orderly, and numbered in the thousands. The
source of visual lecture aids, the second Millerite innovation,
is unknown, though Himes may have played a role. Miller's
calculations in reaching a date for the end point of history
were quite complicated, so Miller and other lecturers made
extensive use of large diagrams. The most common illustra-
tion was a "standard chart" which matched biblical prophecy with human history and had all events point toward the
ominous date at the bottom—"1843."

The purpose of the extensive publicity was to win as
many souls as possible before Jesus returned. To antiformalists, who thrived on emotional revivals, the waves of conversions precipitated by Adventist preaching were further proof

that Miller's message was true. By 1843–1844, the Northern states underwent a new wave of revivalism, a movement largely inspired by the perceived nearness of the Second Coming. Baptist ministers like Elon Galusha warned their listeners that at any time "the song of revelry...will cease; ...the chilling horror will suddenly seize upon you...." Ordinary folk, many of whom already believed in folk apocalyptic, heard commonsense Millerite calculations combined with hellfire and brimstone preaching and raced forward to accept Jesus before God forever closed the doors of heaven. Soon even the skeptical threw themselves on God's mercy, fearing that Miller might be right and that they would be unprepared for Judgment Day. Thus Millerism and revivalism fed on each other as each revival "proved" God's hand was behind Miller's message and each Millerite sermon frightened more sinners into seeking conversion experiences.

It is not surprising that Millerism and revivalism worked so well together. For decades evangelicals had led seekers from the stage of conviction ("you are sinful"), to struggle ("your attempts to save yourself will do no good"), to conversion ("the only hope is to throw yourself on God's mercy and let him act on your life supernaturally"). Miller's message was identical, except it was addressed not only to sinners but to the entire world. Miller argued that the world was sinful, there was nothing humans could do to save it, and hope could come only when Christ reentered history to save the world supernaturally. Miller advised unbelievers to save themselves and to forget a world incapable of redemption. The end could come through death or the Second Coming; in either case the prophet urged sinners to find salvation before it was "too late."

Antiformalists, who distrusted large-scale reform efforts

and who gravitated toward emotional religion, were most affected by the Millerite message. In New York Millerites drew more followers from the Baptists than from any other denomination. In Vermont Adventists drew the bulk of their support from Methodists, Free Will Baptists, and "Christians." Nationally four-fifths of Millerite leaders came from antiformal evangelical churches; by contrast only 9 percent were Congregational and 7 percent Presbyterian. Millerism was strongest in rural areas, particularly in places where farmers were caught in the difficult transition to a national market economy. Miller's followers were not strikingly poor, but compared with the affluent clientele that flocked to Charles Finney, they were not particularly well-off either.

Garrisonian abolitionists also played a significant role in the Millerite crusade. Their presence probably kept Millerism from getting a hearing in Southern antiformal churches where many believed in folk apocalyptic. At first glance "this-worldly" antislavery reformers appear to have had little in common with those awaiting an "other-worldly" return of the Messiah. But Garrisonians and Millerites actually had much in common. Both groups criticized the formal evangelical clergy and extended the Whore of Babylon imagery from the Roman Catholic church to all "established" religion. By 1843 Millerites echoed the earlier Garrisonian plea for the faithful to "come out" from all corrupt churches. Both groups agreed that it was foolish to change the world through human institutions. Like the Garrisonians, some Millerites refused to cast ballots in the 1844 election. Millerite women, like Garrisonian females, were allowed to speak to mixed audiences and assume leadership roles. By the early 1840s Garrisonians found Millerism as hopeful an option as any. Moral suasion had failed, and corruption abounded everywhere. Only a miracle, such as the return of the Lord, could end slavery and perfect human society. Not surprisingly, many Garrisonians opted for Millerism, and when they joined they neglected antislavery agitation in favor of preparing sinners for the Second Coming.

Formal evangelicals, who also disliked the Garrisonians, were William Miller's severest critics. Formalist clergy complained that it was a "sad, dreadful mistake" to believe that "God will bring in the Millennium by a sort of miracle, and chiefly without human agency." Others parodied Miller's calculations: "Multiply the wrinkles upon the horns of a five-year-old ram by the twelve signs of the zodiac, and that product by the number of seeds in a winter squash; you will then find that Gabriel's going to blow next year." Perhaps the most damaging formalist charge was that Miller's doctrine promoted social and mental disorder. Millerite meetings were full of "wild delirium" with "hallooing and wailing until midnight and past," and the Adventist rank and file were marked by "idleness and profligacy." Most ominously, Millerism was responsible for "the worst of all madness—THE MADNESS OF THE SOUL!," a mental condition that could only be reversed by one of the most modern institutions, the insane asylum.

The Millerites' biggest problem was not formalist opposition but the failure of their prophecies. By the early 1830s Miller publicly announced Christ's return "sometime in 1843." Later he modified his statement to refer to "the Jewish year, 1843," which covered the span from March 21, 1843, to March 21, 1844. When March 22, 1844, arrived and Jesus had not yet appeared, many Millerites had a crisis in belief and abandoned the movement. Others saw the apparent failure of prophecy as a time of testing and a "winnowing of the chaff." Having become the laughingstock of their local communities, the remaining Millerites were heartened to read Samuel Snow's article in *The Midnight Cry.* Using the Jewish liturgical calendar as his guide, Snow contended that the Day of Atonement would not occur until October 22, 1844. Suddenly Miller's movement was revitalized. Miller himself overcame his initial reservations and endorsed the October date. On the 22nd Millerites gathered in homes and churches to pray and purify themselves before the Lord's return. Meanwhile non-Millerites watched with anxious skepticism. When the sun rose on October 23 the faithful were again proven wrong, and this time the disillusionment was many times greater.

The failure of Jesus visibly to return on October 22, 1844, became known as the Great Disappointment. William Miller was psychologically shaken by the second prophetic failure. Discouraged by the unhappy results of his life's work, Miller withdrew from public life and died a broken man in 1849. Meanwhile his followers tried to make sense of the failed prophecies. Some continued to argue that the end was near, but, twice burned, they refused to set a date for Christ's return. Others returned to the Scriptures in search of a new date. Still others claimed that the prophecy did not fail, that Jesus came spiritually, and that the doors of salvation were now closed to unbelievers. Eventually some of the remaining believers helped create the Seventh Day Adventist Church, which added diet reform and Saturday worship to an emphasis on the Second Coming.

With the collapse of Millerism after the Great Disappointment, premillennialism lost most of its influence on antiformalists. By 1860 the vast majority of antiformal evangelicals were postmillennialists. Perhaps many antiformalists questioned whether America was truly progressing toward the millennium, but in the absence of a coherent alternative view, these doubts generally remained unexpressed.

*

Unlike white evangelicals, few African American believers accepted the assumptions of postmillennialism. From the black perspective the United States was not getting better; there were many reasons to believe American society was growing worse. After Nat Turner's unsuccessful slave revolt in 1831, Southern laws tightened restrictions on black religion and tried to eliminate slave literacy. The 1850 Fugitive Slave Act endangered Northern African Americans and made it more difficult for Southern blacks to escape the peculiar institution. The Dred Scott decision of 1857 officially denied citizenship to all African Americans and condoned the westward expansion of slavery. Against segregation in Northern cities like Boston and New York there were occasional victories, but for every victory there seemed to be two setbacks somewhere else. Slaves, in particular, found little comfort in postmillennialism. Prominent white millennialists argued that the thousand years would begin far in the distant future (1941 and 2000 were popular dates). Such prophecies brought bondservants no comfort because they placed the millennium (and the end of slavery) far beyond slaves' expected life spans.

The lack of black interest in postmillennialism did not mean that African American evangelicals were unconcerned about the coming of the Lord. Black Christians were generally premillennialists who believed that the Messiah must come before God could establish his reign of righteousness and peace. As in other aspects of the evangelical faith, blacks interpreted the coming of the Lord not only in relation to Scripture but also in relation to slavery and African spirituality. Black evangelicals often referred to the Lord's return as the Day of Jubilee. This phrase originated in ancient Israel's year of jubilee, described in the book of Leviticus.

Every fiftieth year all Hebrew bondservants were freed and all land was returned to its original owners. The Lord warned that if the Hebrews broke their covenant with God by violating the jubilee and other commandments, he would grant the Israelites' adversaries victory and allow heathen nations to ravage Hebrew land. American slavery had existed much longer than fifty years, and therefore God could be expected to destroy white slaveholding, liberate his people, and redistribute the land. This divine retribution was linked to the Second Coming of Christ. But African spirituality shaped the black evangelical understanding of the Second Advent. Instead of hoping for Jesus literally to appear in the sky, blacks expected the Day of the Lord to be a reenactment of the past, when a new tribal hero would replicate the deeds of Samson, Joshua, and Moses, set God's people free, and institute the millennium. And they expected God to act soon. Enslaved blacks, like many premodern peoples, viewed the future as being only a few years ahead. Thus they expected God to break into historical time and provide liberation through a warrior king in the relatively near future. As was true with other aspects of black religion, African American expectations of divine liberation were sung as well as spoken. Spirituals echoed the theme of deliverance—"You'll see de world on fire...see the stars a fallin'...see the moon a bleedin'...see my Jesus coming" —as well as the joys of the millennial kingdom—"Dere's no sun to burn you...no hard trials...no tribulation...All is gladness in de Kingdom."

Most African Americans were expectant premillennialists in that they believed that God would destroy the current social order in his own time without human assistance. Perhaps the means of deliverance were vague, but the hopes for redemption were strong. As the spiritual put it, "O my

Lord deliver'd Daniel, O why not deliver me too?" Even though most black evangelicals shied away from advocating slave revolts, that did not mean they believed God would moderate his wrath against white America. Spirituals contained many images of a wrathful God destroying the social order: "Earth shall reel and totter; Hell shall be uncapped, Th' dragon be loosed," "On th' Day of Judgment—moon turn to blood," and "King Jesus rides on a milk-white horse / No man can hinder him."

While most black evangelicals expectantly waited for God to destroy the peculiar institution, some were revolutionary premillennialists who seized the initiative, assumed a prophetic role, and acted as God's instruments against injustice. The revolutionaries borrowed three key ideas from white antiformalism—literalism, individual biblical interpretation, and folk apocalyptic. The revolutionists' appropriation of these white evangelical elements is not surprising, as the leaders of slave revolts were generally literate, more autonomous than most slaves, and had more contact with white artisans and farmers than did other bondservants. Like all black evangelicals, revolutionists viewed the Bible as a cosmic story in which history was constantly repeated. But they had a tendency to take historical re-creation literally, even to the extent of developing battle plans based on specific Old Testament texts. Some also pointed to "signs" in the heavens as confirmation of their prophetic insights. While meteorological omens may have been part of African religion, they were central to antiformalist folk apocalyptic.

Revolutionary premillennialists led the three major South ern slave revolts or conspiracies between 1800 and 1831. While numerous factors affected the success of each insurrection, evangelicalism clearly played a major role as evangelical thinking legitimized the revolutionaries. Generally speaking, the greater a leader's ability to fulfill Old Testament expectation, the greater his ability to unify and direct his Bible-believing followers.

The year 1800 was pivotal in the lives of three revolutionary leaders, men Gayraud Wilmore has described as "Three Generals in the Lord's Army." In 1800 Gabriel Prosser attempted a revolt near Richmond, Virginia, Denmark Vesey purchased his freedom, and Nat Turner was born. The efforts of these three men shaped black revolutionary premillennialism.

Inspired by the successful Haitian revolution led by Toussaint L'Ouverture seven years earlier, Gabriel Prosser in the summer of 1800 recruited fellow bondsmen for a massive attack on Virginian slavery. Slave-artisans assumed the leadership of the planned revolt because of their literacy, greater freedom of movement, and understanding of the region's resources and geography. Having spent the month of August enlisting field hands, Gabriel Prosser decided that Saturday, August 30, would be an excellent night to attack the state capital. Prosser hoped that news of the attack on Richmond would stimulate slaves to rise spontaneously against their masters throughout Virginia. In the face of such an onslaught, demoralized whites would grant enslaved African Americans their freedom. Unfortunately for Prosser's insurrection, a torrential downpour that washed away a key bridge on the road to Richmond made it impossible to carry out the attack on August 30. He delayed the mission until Sunday, August 31—but by Sunday several slaves had informed their masters of the planned revolt. Whites began to round up conspirators, and Prosser was forced to flee by ship, only to be betrayed by slave crewmen on the vessel in which he was traveling. By mid-October Gabriel Prosser and thirty-five other slaves had been hanged for their roles in the abortive rebellion.

To a large degree evangelical Christianity inspired the leaders of insurrection. Gabriel Prosser admired Samson, one of the great judges of ancient Israel, and, like his hero, wore his hair long. Just as Samson slew the Philistines after "the Spirit of the Lord came mightily upon him," Prosser believed God would empower him to overturn slavery and establish a new black kingdom in Virginia. Prosser's brother, Martin, was a preacher who related Old Testament passages to insurrection strategy. Even though scholars agree that evangelical views played a role in Prosser's rebellion, there is considerable disagreement over whether Christianity was central to the planned revolt. Some historians contend that while Prosser himself was inspired by evangelical views, he inadvertently weakened his appeal to field hands by describing the revolt in practical rather than religious terms. Others question the depth of Prosser's religious convictions, contending that liberty was Prosser's only religion. Recent studies have reiterated what black religious scholars have been saying for several decades: that African American Christianity has been intimately involved in promoting black radicalism, such as Gabriel's Insurrection, from the early years of the Republic.

There is more agreement on Denmark Vesey's 1822 conspiracy in South Carolina since historians recognize that Vesey drew heavily on evangelical as well as African religion. Vesey bought his freedom in 1800 with money received from winning the East-Bay-Street Lottery. His good fortune came when he was in his early thirties, and while his prize was substantial, it was not great enough to purchase freedom for his children. For nearly two decades Vesey spoke out against slavery but did little more. By 1817, however, changes in local religious life opened the door of opportunity. Following the lead of Richard Allen, Charleston's black Methodists withdrew from the city's white churches and formed several African Methodist Episcopal congregations. In 1818, 140 members of the Hampstead AME church were arrested for unlawful assembly, a bishop and four ministers were sentenced to one month in prison or exile from the state, and eight other ministers were sentenced to ten lashes or a fine of ten dollars. Vesey, a member of the Hampstead congregation, sought to turn the black evangelicals' anger into revolutionary action. By 1822 Vesey, key African religionists (such as Gullah Jack, a noted conjurer), and numerous African Methodists had developed a plan. On June 16 hundreds of blacks would move on signal and raid the city's arsenal and gun shops. The conspirators would kill all whites on sight (with the exception of "several white men of low character" who were part of the conspiracy) and set fire to the city. Once slaves in the country heard of the black conquest of Charleston, they would also rise against their masters, thus setting off a revolution that would destroy South Carolinian slavery forever.

Like Gabriel Prosser, Denmark Vesey never had a chance to put his plan into action. In late May one of the slaves recruited for the rebellion informed his master, who then alerted Charleston authorities to the upcoming danger. One hundred thirty-one persons were arrested, of whom forty-three were exiled from South Carolina and thirty-seven, including Vesey, were executed. Vesey's "revolt" was more explicitly evangelical than was the earlier insurrection attempt by Prosser. Although Vesey was assisted by Gullah Jack, who claimed he could not be killed by whites and who threatened to cast an evil spell on anyone betraying the revolt, it is clear that Vesey himself operated within an

African American evangelical framework. Like most black
believers, Vesey preferred the Old Testament, saw African
Americans as God's chosen people, and expected slavery to
end in a violent cataclysm when God reenacted Exodus to
save his nation. Unlike most black believers, Vesey interpreted the Old Testament quite literally, using the Book of
Joshua to plan his battle strategies. Vesey realized that
Charleston revolutionaries, like the ancient Israelites, faced
overwhelming odds in fighting their enemy. But Vesey was
convinced that God would give his people the victory. Like
Joshua, Vesey commanded his followers to kill every enemy
man, woman, or child whom they encountered and then
utterly destroy the city in which the enemy had lived.
Exceptions were made for the few whites who were in on
the plot, an act that paralleled Joshua's protection of Rahab
and her household. It is not coincidental that Vesey's original
attack date, July 14, and his second and final choice, June 16,
both fell on the Christian Sabbath, just as Joshua's victory
over Jericho occurred on the Jewish Sabbath. In each case
God's chosen people expected Jehovah to use his holy day to
cleanse the land of iniquity and to prepare the promised
land for his people.

The largest slave revolt in American history, Nat Turner's
Rebellion, occurred in Southampton County, Virginia, in
1831. Like the earlier rebellions, this insurrection was led by
a literate black with a significant degree of personal freedom, a man who had studied the Scriptures independently
and concluded that he was called by God to liberate his
people. Frustrated by demeaning field labor and angered by
the degradation of his people, Turner became convinced
through a series of visions, omens, and signs that Jehovah
called him to destroy slavery. On Sunday, August 21, 1831,
Turner and six other slaves put their plan into action. Turner

began the revolt with these few loyal assistants rather than enlisting large numbers beforehand and risking betrayal as other black revolutionaries had done. Early Monday morning Turner's band struck his master's household, killing all seven members. Then the insurrectionists moved on, killing all whites they met and gathering weapons, provisions, and new recruits as they advanced toward the Southampton County seat, Jerusalem. By noon Monday Turner's men had killed almost sixty whites, their numbers had grown to about seventy troops, and they had advanced within three miles of their objective when they were intercepted by a party of white volunteer militiamen who succeeded in driving Turner's outnumbered and disorganized forces into Virginia's dense forests. Soon Turner's forces were in disarray. If Turner had instigated a "black terror," local vigilantes created a "white terror" of their own, killing captured revolutionaries and at least 120 blacks who had nothing to do with the revolt. Eventually fifty blacks were tried and twenty-one, including Turner, were hanged for their role in the insurrection.

Nat Turner's spirituality was clearly in the African American evangelical tradition. Like many black Protestants, Turner consciously rejected voodoo but retained religious beliefs from the African past. Soon after Nat was born, his family noticed he had peculiar birthmarks, signs that he had the intellectual gifts of a "witcheh-man." Turner's Methodist grandmother, Bridget, fostered Nat's spiritual growth, encouraged him to spend time in prayer and meditation, and reinforced his belief that God had made him for a great purpose. When Turner was in his late teens he heard a voice in the wind repeat the words of Jesus—"Seek ye the kingdom of Heaven and all things shall be added unto you." A few years later the words of God were reinforced by a series of visions, followed by a number of mysterious natural signs. In the late 1820s Turner said he discovered blood on some corn, which he claimed was Jesus' blood "returning to earth again in the form of dew." He also claimed to have found strange hieroglyphic characters etched on leaves in nearby woods "and numbers, with the forms of men in different attitudes, portrayed in blood." On May 12, 1828, the Spirit appeared to Turner and urged him to assume Christ's yoke "and fight against the Serpent, for the time was fast approaching when the first should be last and the last should be first." The implication of the vision was clear: God had called Turner to strike down the Serpent, slavery. But he was reluctant to act until Jehovah had further verified his will through additional signs. Despite his caution Turner clearly believed he was the new Moses, called by God to set his people free.

Other aspects of Turner's spirituality, such as his individualism, resembled white antiformalism. This parallel is not surprising as Turner's childhood master, Benjamin Turner, was a staunch Methodist, encouraged Nat to read the Bible, and brought Nat to prayer meetings in the local biracial Methodist church. Not content to accept white interpretations of Holy Writ and possessing the powers of literacy, Turner, like many antiformalists before him, sought the true meaning of Scripture through individual study. By 1825 he dropped out of slave society, avoided praise meetings, and spent his Sundays alone in intense prayer and Bible study. When he emerged from this period of withdrawal he announced that God had spoken to him in a series of visions. Such an approach ran contrary to usual African American methods of biblical interpretation, which emphasized the preaching, singing, and interpreting of the Word as a community.

Turner was not only individualistic, he shared antiformalist folk apocalyptic. Like many whites, he searched the
heavens for divine messages and believed unusual meteorological events were omens of the end times. While it is
impossible to determine whether interpretive sky-watching
began with Europeans or Africans, it is likely that in
America both cultures reinforced the practice. In February
1831 a solar eclipse, which also alarmed many whites,
provided the sign Turner had requested. On August 12,
1831, during the "Three Blue Days," Turner believed he saw
a black hand appear to cross the sun, an event that had a
clear interpretation: "as the black spot passed over the sun,
so shall the black pass over the earth." Now that God had
given his celestial signs, Turner believed the Coming of the
Lord and the Day of Jubilee were at hand.

After 1831 African American slaves favored expectant
over revolutionary premillennialism. Southern whites responded to the Turner Rebellion by enacting further legal
restrictions on slave literacy and by increasing their supervision of black religion, hoping to prevent the rise of future
black messianic leaders. Noting the failure of Turner's revolt
and increased white surveillance, most black evangelicals left
the details of the Day of Jubilee to the Lord. In the
meantime slaves continued day-by-day rebellion on a much
smaller scale. Bondservants resisted through work slow-
downs, breaking tools, stealing from the master, and violating plantation rules. They also assisted runaways, spiriting
fellow slaves northward as they sought to redeem their
brothers and sisters one soul at a time. The lack of major
slave revolts between 1831 and 1861 did not signify a
lessening in premillennial ardor. Instead the relative quiet
suggests that Southern blacks placed their freedom as a
people in the hands of Jehovah. In emancipation, as in

salvation, slaves recognized that the Lord was a "time-God" who "won't make haste."

Millennialism continued to have an enormous influence over the United States on the eve of the Civil War. When the great conflict came, Americans spoke of the war using millennial language. Having been steeped in biblical prophecy and apocalyptic images for decades, it is not surprising that the Civil War generation described the conflict in Armageddon-like terms and tried to fit current events into a broader prophetic context. Northern whites, Southern whites, and African Americans all used their understanding of prophecy and God's role in history to make sense of the four years of carnage.

At the beginning of the war most Northerners believed that the American system of government was God's tool for bringing the millennium to the world; preserving the Union therefore had to be the nation's highest political goal. Philadelphia clergyman Henry Boardman articulated this view: "The Union is too sacred a trust to be sacrificed except upon the most imperative grounds...it is too closely linked with the cause of human liberty, and with the salvation of the world. To destroy it at the bidding of passion; to destroy it until every practicable means for preserving it has been tried and exhausted, would be a crime of appalling turpitude against patriotism, against religion, and against humanity."

By late 1861 casualties were mounting, the Union army had suffered a series of setbacks, and hopes for an early restoration of the Union were vanishing. The Civil War was not a minor interruption on the way to the millennium but a tribulation of catastrophic proportions. Northerners pondered the meaning of the extended conflict and concluded that the Almighty was chastising his chosen people for their sins. Preachers and laypersons searched their lives to find the evil that so angered the Almighty. When the lists of wrong-doing were compiled, one sin stood above all the rest. In his second inaugural address, Lincoln described the war as divine punishment: "If God wills that [the war] continue until all the wealth piled up by the bondman's two hundred and fifty years of unrequited toil shall be sunk, and until every drop drawn with the lash shall be paid by another drawn with the sword, as was said three thousand years ago, so still it must be said, 'The judgments of the Lord are true and righteous altogether.'"

The pain of seemingly unending conflict focused the North's attention on slavery in a way that black and white abolitionists had never accomplished. Within the rhetoric of postmillennialism, the North had only two choices: genu-inely repent by destroying Southern slavery or continue to suffer the wrath of the Almighty. Initially Lincoln, who feared losing border states to the Confederacy, rejected any linkage between the war and emancipation. But when the president began to search for meaning in the nation's ordeal, he questioned his earlier position. In the summer of 1862 Lincoln asked God for a sign. While waiting for news regarding the Battle of Antietam, the president made a covenant with Jehovah: if the Union army defeated Lee, Lincoln would take that as a sign that the Almighty wanted the slaves to be free. When the Union forces were victorious at Antietam, Lincoln fulfilled his part of the bargain and announced the Emancipation Proclamation, claiming "God had decided this question in favor of the slaves."

When the North redefined the war's purpose it turned the conflict into a millennial crusade shared by evangelicals and nonevangelicals alike. The cause of the Union had been transformed into the cause of God. Julia Ward Howe, a

Boston abolitionist who was by no means an evangelical, captured this apocalyptic zeal brilliantly in "The Battle Hymn of the Republic." Not surprisingly, she used millennial rhetoric to portray the North's new sense of purpose. The first, fourth, and fifth verses read:

> Mine eyes have seen the glory of the coming of the Lord:
> He is trampling out the vintage where the grapes of wrath are stored;
> He hath loosed the fateful lightning of his terrible swift sword:
> His truth is marching on.
>
> He has sounded forth the trumpet that shall never call retreat;
> He is sifting out the hearts of men before His judgment-seat;
> Oh, be swift, my soul, to answer him! be jubilant, my feet!
> Our God is marching on.
>
> In the beauty of the lilies Christ was born across the sea,
> With a glory in his bosom that transfigures you and me:
> As he died to make men holy, let us die to make men free,
> While God is marching on.

While blue-clad troops were marching to the tune of the millennium, Southern pulpits rang with apocalyptic rhetoric, for the Confederacy also understood itself to be furthering the cause of God. Richard Fuller, president of the Southern Baptist Convention, declared in 1861 that "every principle of religion, of patriotism, and of humanity calls upon us to pledge our fortunes and our lives" to drive back the "savage barbarity" of the North. A Presbyterian minister argued that the South was the new Israel and that Lincoln was the incarnation of Pharaoh: "Eleven tribes sought to go forth in peace from the house of political bondage, but the heart of our modern Pharaoh is hardened, that he will not let Israel go."

As in the North, prolonged conflict led to a reassessment of the South's position. As the war dragged on it was not at all clear that God was on the Confederate side. Rather than viewing the war as a vindication of the Southern way of life, many groups saw it as the "hand of God" punishing the South for its sins. Like Northerners, Southern whites believed that slavery was the source of Jehovah's displeasure. But repentant Confederates did not repudiate the peculiar institution, they only repented of misusing slavery. God was punishing the South because many slaveowners pursued profits to the exclusion of Christianizing and civilizing the slaves. A *Confederate Union* essayist complained that white laws curtailing slave literacy, which kept many blacks from reading the Bible, were "one of the many reasons why God is withholding...his smiles from the righteous struggles we are waging with our cruel foes." A Georgia reformer wrote that Southern whites had made slavery "a stumbling block over which men fall into hell," and that the errors within the existing system of bondage "must be speedily corrected or God will blot us out from among the nations of the earth." Even as defeat piled on defeat later in the war, many white Southerners contended that slavery was "a grand civilizing and Christianizing school," and that they only needed to ask God's forgiveness for not having done more for the slaves, not for having enslaved Africans in the first place.

African Americans saw the millennial potential of the Civil War from the time the first shots were fired at Fort Sumter. Generations of black evangelicals had prophesied

that God would destroy the peculiar institution, and in 1861
Judgment Day was close at hand. Blacks followed the course
of the conflict with great interest, anxiously watching the
angel of the Lord pass over the South and bring liberty to
God's people and destruction to his foes. A few even used
literalist scriptural interpretation to show how God had
promised a Northern victory. When the Civil War brought
the promised freedom, black evangelicals interpreted slavery's demise in ways consistent with their eschatology. God
had raised a deliverer who set his people free. Former slave
Mingo White exclaimed, "The children of Israel was in
bondage one time, and God sent Moses to 'liver them. Well
I s'pose that God sent Abe Lincoln to 'liver us." After
Lincoln's assassination the connection between the president
and earlier heroes became clearer. A South Carolinian
remarked, "Lincoln died for we, Christ died for we, and
me believe him de same mans." When a Union officer
visited a freedmen's school and asked, "Children, who is
Jesus Christ?" the consensus response was "Massa Linkum."
A black preacher referred to the slain president as "Massa
Linkum! our 'dored Redeemer an' Saviour an' Frien'!"
Black expectant premillennialists had predicted that God
would raise up a new Moses-Jesus to free his people, and
their prophecies were fulfilled. The Day of Jubilee had come
and ex-slaves throughout the South sang, "I's free, I's free,
I's free at las'! Thank God A'mighty, I's free at las'!"

The Day of Jubilee had arrived. Yet the ensuing millennium was a disappointment. For a brief period of time
under congressional Reconstruction, black men received
their political rights and used the right to vote to improve
their civil condition. But the land redistribution that came
with the Hebrew jubilee did not occur in the United States.
Without their "forty acres and a mule," the bare minimum

for financial independence, freedmen lacked the economic base necessary to protect their political and social liberties. Gradually the promised years of peace and prosperity deteriorated into lynchings, debt peonage, and Jim Crow laws.

Epilogue

BETWEEN 1820 and 1865 evangelicals had an enormous influence on American culture. Their emphasis on reading the Bible encouraged literacy, created support for public education, and led to the formation of dozens of American colleges. The desire to flood the nation with religious literature encouraged evangelicals to use innovative printing and bureaucratic techniques which were later adopted by secular presses and organizations. The belief in emotional conversions spread far beyond the boundaries of evangelicalism as other Christian groups experimented with enthusiastic religion and as devotionalism promoted sentimentality in the larger middle-class culture. Likewise, evangelical perfectionism had secular parallels such as diet reform, the water cure, phrenology, and communitarianism, all of which were attempts at perfecting American life. Evangelical disputes often spread into the political arena—Sabbatarianism, temperance, and abolitionism all helped shape partisan alignments in the political party systems. Finally, all Americans tended to use evangelical millennial rhetoric to make sense of the Civil War.

But cultural change was not a one-way street. Between 1820 and 1865 American evangelicalism was itself transformed by urbanization, secularization, and sectionalism. By the end of the Civil War evangelicals were still divided into formalist, antiformalist, and African American camps. Precise patterns are difficult to trace, however, as formalist/antiformalist divisions within denominations gradually became as important as the differences between denominations. Overall the three groups had a different composition in 1865 compared with 1820.

After the Civil War, formalists included Congregationalists, a number of other Calvinist groups, and evangelical Episcopalians as well as many Northern Presbyterians, Baptists, Methodists, and Disciples. These groups all sought an orderly faith, preferred decorous and structured worship, revered education, gravitated toward institutional solutions for national problems, and were close to the center of national power. Among all formalist groups, these trends were strongest for those living in America's cities. Northern urban Baptists, Methodists, and Disciples were relative newcomers to post–Civil War formalism. Since the 1830s they had increasingly emphasized education for both clergy and laypersons, sophistication rather than enthusiasm in worship, and bureaucratized benevolence. As they grew in wealth and status, large numbers abandoned the Democrats and joined the Republicans. After experiencing denominational schisms, the Union Prayer Meeting Revival, and the Civil War, many middle-and upper-class Northern evangelicals realized they had more in common with those of a different denomination who worshiped down the street than they had with Southerners who shared their theological tradition.

After 1865 formalist groups gradually split into competing factions, thus eroding the spirit of cooperation that had made the antebellum benevolent empire possible. Before the Civil War formal evangelicals believed that America was the New Israel, that God expected Christians to redeem the social order, and that each individual had to experience personal conversion in order to be saved. By the 1880s three groups had emerged, each believing part of the earlier formal evangelical world view but none accepting formalist thinking in its entirety. Ministers in the first group believed America was the New Israel but placed little emphasis on saving either souls or society. Instead clergymen in wealthy urban congregations often glorified the capitalist system, preached a Christianized form of Social Darwinism known as the gospel of wealth, and announced that prosperity signified divine approval. A second formalist group maintained the antebellum emphasis on redeeming American society. Well aware of the human misery in urban factories and slums, these formalists rejected the gospel of wealth and proclaimed the social gospel, a doctrine that argued that Christians were supposed to heal suffering in this world and not just try to save souls for the world to come. The third formalist group emphasized individual salvation, supported interdenominational evangelistic agencies, and advocated large-scale urban revivals. While Dwight Moody, the era's most famous evangelist, emphasized the planning and organization of evangelism, he had few programmatic solutions for America's urban problems. Moody did not oppose the social gospel; he just did not think that efforts at reform would accomplish much. As a premillennialist, Moody believed that trying to save society would do little good and that his primary responsibility was to try to save as many souls as possible before Jesus returned. Eventually Moody's followers would find themselves more comfortable among antiformalists, who also emphasized evangelism rather than wide-scale social reform.

As the century closed, divisions among the three formalist groups grew sharper, and formal evangelicalism lost much its ability to shape and control American culture. By 1908, when the formalists spearheaded the creation of a new interdenominational agency, the Federal Council of Churches, the social gospel advocates were the most powerful of the three formalist groups. Middle-of-the-road evangelicalism was well on its way to becoming mainline Protestantism.

After 1865 antiformalists included many Southern and rural Presbyterians, Baptists, Methodists, and Disciples, as well as holiness advocates dissatisfied with the growing formalism in both Northern and Southern Protestant denominations. Southern Presbyterians were the major newcomers to the antiformal group, as mutual participation in the Confederate "lost cause" overrode earlier class antagonisms with Southern Baptists, Methodists, and Disciples. In both the North and South small holiness groups (such as the Salvation Army and Methodist holiness activists who eventually formed the Church of the Nazarene) were active in antiformal circles. In addition, rural evangelicals, alarmed at the erosion of traditional values in wealthy, prestigious, highly educated urban congregations, clung ardently to antiformalism.

In general, antiformal evangelicals retained most of their pre–Civil War characteristics. Antiformalists had always interpreted Scripture literally. After some Northern formalists reevaluated traditional teaching in light of Darwinism and higher criticism, antiformalists increased their opposition to Northern seminaries and advocated a doctrine of biblical inerrancy. Antiformal evangelicals continued to stress personal conversion, and many were open to Phoebe Palmer's holiness teaching. As earlier, antiformalists continued to favor private charity or local governmental efforts to address social problems. Holiness groups such as the Salvation Army pursued a privatized version of the social gospel by avoiding political action and providing charity and the gospel direct to the poor.

Several groups had new reasons to see themselves as antiformalist after 1865. White Southerners, who lost the Civil

War and saw themselves as culturally and politically marginalized by the dominant North, had little reason to believe that the world was gradually getting better. Holiness groups felt out of place within middle-class Methodism. Rural Northerners, who saw the farm economy shrink in significance, and Old School Presbyterians, whose theological education now seemed out of date, also moved in an antiformal direction. Not surprisingly, Southern whites, holiness advocates, rural Northerners, and Old School Presbyterians showed renewed interest in premillennialism after the Civil War. Eventually three sets of ideas—premillennialism, holiness teaching, and Old School Presbyterianism—would coalesce into twentieth-century fundamentalism.

African Americans had a brief period of political and social liberty after 1865 but then saw their position erode as a system of legalized segregation limited black opportunities in the South, the border states, and portions of the North. Even where segregation was not officially practiced, racial prejudice limited opportunities, and the black community again had to draw on its own resources for survival. In the North and in the South, black evangelical churches provided the foundation of African American culture, the black ministry attracted many of the most talented leaders within the community, and the black evangelical faith sustained the African American people in the face of ongoing adversity.

In the years after the Civil War American evangelicalism lost much of its earlier cultural impact. Formal evangelicalism weakened in the face of scientific and intellectual advances. Some formalists left the evangelical camp altogether while others tried to reconcile evangelicalism to the latest scientific discoveries. Among the well educated, evangelicalism was losing its appeal. Lower-class antiformalists had likewise lost control over American culture. Most white antiformalists lived in the South, were the losers in the Civil War, and were generally in social and political retreat. African American evangelicals did not dominate American culture either. As racial violence and social discrimination increased, black evangelicals saw survival, rather than cultural influence, as their goal. The evangelical era had ended. New forces, those of modernization, industrialization, and secularization, would dominate the United States after the Civil War.

A Note on Sources

RATHER THAN LISTING more than two hundred primary and secondary works consulted in the course of preparing this book, I describe here the works that have had the greatest impact on my thinking.

A number of general works on American religion were highly useful. For encyclopedic detail on various religious movements and leading figures, see Sydney Ahlstrom, *A Religious History of the American People* (Garden City, N.Y., 1975). Mark Noll, Nathan Hatch, George Marsden, David Wells, and John Woodbridge, *Christianity in America: A Handbook* (Grand Rapids, Mich., 1983) is a carefully structured collection of short essays which together cover a huge portion of America's religious history. Mark Noll, *A History of Christianity in the United States and Canada* (Grand Rapids, Mich., 1992) is comprehensive, accessible, and current. For a persuasive and systematic overview of American religious evolution, turn to William McLoughlin, *Revivals, Awakenings, and Reform: An Essay on Religion and Social Change in America, 1607–1977* (Chicago, 1978). Jon Butler, *Awash in a Sea of Faith: Christianizing the American People* (Cambridge, Mass., 1990) traces the nation's religious history from the early colonial period to the Civil War. Martin Marty, *Righteous Empire: The Protestant Experience in America* (New York, 1970) covers Protestantism from the American Revolution to the 1950s.

Turning to more specific topics, Roger Finke and Rodney Stark, "How the Upstart Sects Won America: 1776–1850,"

Journal for the Scientific Study of Religion 28 (1989): 27–44, provides a splendid overview of why the antiformalists were more successful recruiters than the formalists. For a discussion of the African American role in the evangelical tradition, see Milton Sernett, "Black Religion and the Question of Evangelical Identity," in Donald Dayton and Robert Johnston, eds., *The Variety of American Evangelicalism* (Knoxville, Tenn., 1991). Statistical information on denominational memberships and populations comes from Finke and Stark, "Upstart Sects"; Robert Baird, *Religion in America* (New York, 1856); George Marsden, *Religion and American Culture* (San Diego, 1990); and Albert Raboteau, *Slave Religion: The "Invisible Institution" in the Antebellum South* (New York, 1978).

A number of books provide excellent analyses of formal, antiformal, and black evangelicalism. My thinking about formalists was heavily influenced by Daniel Walker Howe, "The Evangelical Movement and Political Culture in the North During the Second Party System," *Journal of American History* 77 (1991): 1216–1239. Richard Rabinowitz, *The Spiritual Self in Everyday Life: The Transformation of Personal Religious Experience in Nineteenth-Century New England* (Boston, 1989) is a splendid investigation of the internal world of New England formalists. Fred Hood, *Reformed America: The Middle and Southern States, 1783–1837* (University, Ala., 1980), and John Kuykendall, *Southern Enterprize: The Work of National Evangelical Societies in the Antebellum South* (Westport, Conn., 1982) both describe benevolence activity outside New England. The best introduction to antiformalism is Nathan Hatch, *The Democratization of American Christianity* (New Haven, 1989). For discussions of antimissionism, see Bertram Wyatt-Brown, "The Antimission Movement in the Jacksonian South: A Study in Regional Folk

Culture," *Journal of Southern History* 36 (1970): 501–529, and
Byron Cecil Lambert, *The Rise of the Anti-Mission Baptists:
Sources and Leaders, 1800–1840* (New York, 1980). For an
introduction to the thought and culture of the Disciples of
Christ, read David Edwin Harrell, Jr., *Quest for a Christian
America: The Disciples of Christ and American Society to 1866*
(Nashville, Tenn., 1966). Emory Bucke, ed., *The History of
American Methodism* (New York, 1964) is an essential re-
source for studying the spiritual descendants of John Wesley.
The Africanness of black religion is a central argument in
Sterling Stuckey, *Slave Culture: Nationalist Theory and the
Foundations of Black America* (New York, 1987). Raboteau's
Slave Religion argues that black religion was a synthesis of
Christian belief and African practice. Milton Sernett, *Black
Religion and American Evangelicalism: White Protestants, Plan-
tation Missions, and the Flowering of Negro Christianity, 1787–1865*
(Metuchen, N.J., 1975), and Mechal Sobel, *Trabelin' On: The
Slave Journey to an Afro-Baptist Faith* (Westport, Conn., 1979)
are rich overviews of the evolution of black Christianity in
the antebellum South. The cultural aspects of black religion
are discussed in C. Eric Lincoln and Lawrence Mamiya, *The
Black Church in the African American Experience* (Durham,
N.C., 1990); Eugene Genovese, *Roll, Jordan, Roll: The World
the Slaves Made* (New York, 1976); and Lawrence Levine,
*Black Culture and Black Consciousness: Afro-American Folk
Thought from Slavery to Freedom* (New York, 1977). For the
role of African American ministers, see David Swift, *Black
Prophets of Justice: Activist Clergy Before the Civil War* (Baton
Rouge, La., 1989).

Regional and local studies enriched the arguments in this
book. See Mary Ryan, *Cradle of the Middle Class: The Family
in Oneida County, New York, 1790–1865* (Cambridge, Mass.,
1981); Paul Johnson, *A Shopkeeper's Millennium: Society and*

Revivals in Rochester, New York, 1815–1837 (New York, 1978); and Curtis Johnson, *Islands of Holiness: Rural Religion in Upstate New York, 1790–1860* (Ithaca, 1989) for three local studies of New York communities. Randolph Roth, *The Democratic Dilemma: Religion, Reform, and the Social Order in the Connecticut River Valley of Vermont, 1791–1850* (Cambridge, Mass., 1987) is a comprehensive study of interacting religious groups in the eastern half of Vermont. P. Jeffrey Potash, *Vermont's Burned-Over District: Patterns of Community Development and Religious Activity, 1761–1850* (Brooklyn, N.Y., 1991) is also useful for Vermont's religious history. Donald Mathews, *Religion in the Old South* (Chicago, 1977) discusses the interrelationship between black and white evangelicalism in the antebellum South. John Boles, *Religion in Antebellum Kentucky* (Lexington, Ky., 1976) and Bill Cecil-Fronsman, *Common Whites: Class and Culture in Antebellum North Carolina* (Lexington, Ky., 1992) are two helpful state studies. For the white Southern ministry, see Anne Loveland, *Southern Evangelicals and the Social Order, 1800–1860* (Baton Rouge, La., 1980), and E. Brooks Holifield, *The Gentleman Theologians: American Theology in Southern Culture, 1795–1860* (Durham, N.C., 1978).

A number of autobiographies and biographies were particularly helpful. W. P. Strickland edited two important volumes, *Autobiography of Peter Cartwright: The Backwoods Preacher* (New York, 1856) and *Autobiography of Rev. James B. Finley or, Pioneer Life in the West* (Cincinnati, 1856). The autobiographies of Frederick Douglass and Harriet Jacobs are in Henry Louis Gates, Jr., ed., *The Classic Slave Narratives* (New York, 1987). For a short biography of Charles Finney, see William McLoughlin, *Modern Revivalism: Charles Grandison Finney to Billy Graham* (New York, 1959).

1. PEOPLE OF THE WORD

For an introduction to the importance of the Bible in Protestant thought, see Nathan Hatch and Mark Noll, eds., *The Bible in America: Essays in Cultural History* (New York, 1982). David Reynolds, "From Doctrine to Narrative: The Rise of Pulpit Storytelling in America," *America Quarterly* 32 (1980): 479–498, describes the evolution of antebellum preaching. For a discussion of the impact of Scottish Common Sense Realism, read Mark Noll, "Common Sense Traditions and American Evangelical Thought," *American Quarterly* 37 (1985): 216–238. John MacPherson, *The Westminster Confession of Faith* (Edinburgh, 1977) is a thorough explanation of the doctrinal foundation of American Calvinism. Clifford Griffin, *Their Brothers' Keepers: Moral Stewardship in the United States, 1800–1865* (New Brunswick, N.J., 1960) is a classic overview of the formalist benevolent empire. Carl Kaestle, *Pillars of the Republic: Common Schools and American Society, 1780–1860* (New York, 1983) explains the development of the antebellum public school movement. Mary McDougall Gordon, "Patriots and Christians: A Reassessment of Nineteenth-Century School Reformers," *Journal of Social History* 11 (1978): 554–573, reexamines the motivations of those promoting Massachusetts school reform. For a classic description of the importance of evangelicals to the formation of antebellum colleges, see Donald Tewksbury, *The Founding of American Colleges and Universities Before the Civil War* (New York, 1932). The best treatment of Sabbath education is Anne Boylan, *Sunday School: The Formation of an American Institution, 1790–1880* (New Haven, 1988). For an introduction to African American sermons, read Henry Mitchell, *Black Preaching* (Philadelphia, 1970). Slave literacy is thoroughly discussed in Janet Duitsman Cornelius, *"When*

I Can Read My Title Clear": Literacy, Slavery, and Religion in the Antebellum South (Columbia, S.C., 1991). Leon Litwack, *North of Slavery: The Negro in the Free States, 1790–1860* (Chicago, 1961) portrays the barriers in African American advancement in the antebellum North and includes numerous examples of discrimination in education. For the evangelical impact on publishing, see David Paul Nord, "The Evangelical Origins of Mass Media in America, 1815–1835," *Journalism Monographs* 88 (1984): 1–30.

2. THE SECOND BIRTH

For an overview of the process of conversion and the impact of the conversion paradigm on American literature, see Peter Dorsey, *Sacred Estrangement: The Rhetoric of Conversion in Modern American Autobiography* (forthcoming). The first chapter of Richard Carwardine, *Trans-Atlantic Revivalism: Popular Evangelicalism in Britain and America, 1790–1865* (Westport, Conn., 1978) is an excellent overview of New Measures revivalism. Frontier religion is portrayed in Paul Conkin, *Cane Ridge: America's Pentecost* (Madison, Wisc., 1990); John Boles, *The Great Revival, 1787–1805* (Lexington, Ky., 1972); Charles Johnson, *The Frontier Camp Meeting: Religion's Harvest Time* (Dallas, 1955); and Dickson Bruce, *And They All Sang Hallelujah: Plain-Folk Camp-Meeting Religion, 1800–1845* (Knoxville, Tenn., 1974). The best anthology of black conversion narratives is George Rawick, general ed., *The American Slave: A Composite Autobiography* (Series Two, 12 Vols., Westport, Conn., 1972), Vol. 19, *God Struck Me Dead* (Fisk University). William Ferris, Jr., "The Negro Conversion," *Keystone Folklore Quarterly* 15 (1970): 35–51, is a perceptive interpretation of the African American conversion experience. For a comparative study of black and poor white conversions, see Dickson Bruce, "Religion, Society and Culture in the Old South: A Comparative View," *American Quarterly* 25 (1974): 399–416. See Don Yoder, "The Bench Versus the Catechism: Revivalism and Pennsylvania's Lutheran and Reformed Churches," *Pennsylvania Folklife* 10 (1959): 14–23, and Jay Dolan, *Catholic Revivalism: The American Experience, 1830–1900* (Notre Dame, Ind., 1978) for discussions of Lutheran and Catholic revivalism.

3. A JUST AND HOLY LIFE

Barbara Welter's essays, "The Cult of True Womanhood, 1800–1860," and "The Feminization of American Religion, 1800–1860," in *Dimity Convictions: The American Woman in the Nineteenth Century* (Athens, Ohio, 1976), are essential to understanding the religious world of nineteenth-century women. For a more recent discussion of antebellum domesticity, see A. Gregory Schneider, "Social Religion, the Christian Home, and Republican Spirituality in Antebellum Methodism," *Journal of the Early Republic* 10 (1990): 163–189. The maternal associations are discussed in Richard Meckel, "Educating a Ministry of Mothers: Evangelical Maternal Associations, 1815–1860," *Journal of the Early Republic* 2 (1982): 403–423. For holiness, read Timothy Smith, *Revivalism and Social Reform: American Protestantism on the Eve of the Civil War* (New York, 1957); Lucille Dayton and Donald Dayton, " 'Your Daughters Shall Prophesy': Feminism in the Holiness Movement," *Methodist History* 14 (1976): 67–92; and Melvin Easterday Dieter, *The Holiness Revival of the Nineteenth Century* (Metuchen, N.J., 1980). For a short essay on Phoebe Palmer, see Anne Loveland, "Domesticity and Religion in the Antebellum Period: The

Career of Phoebe Palmer," *The Historian* 39 (1977): 455–471. For an example of formalist female perfectionist activism, see Nancy Hewitt, *Women's Activism and Social Change: Rochester, New York, 1822–1872* (Ithaca, 1984). Cortland Victor Smith, "Church Organization as an Agency of Social Control: Church Discipline in North Carolina, 1800–1860 (Ph.D. dissertation, University of North Carolina, 1967) contains a wealth of information on Southern discipline. Other forms of American perfectionism are discussed in Ronald Walters, *American Reformers, 1815–1860* (New York, 1978).

4. God's Chosen People

Any discussion of America as the New Israel must begin with Robert Bellah's famous essay, "Civil Religion in America," which is reprinted in Russell Richey and Donald Jones, eds., *American Civil Religion* (New York, 1974). For Bellah's later thinking on this topic, read *The Broken Covenant* (New York, 1975). The intersection of Christian and political thought during the Revolution is explored in Nathan Hatch, *The Sacred Cause of Liberty: Republican Thought and the Millennium in Revolutionary New England* (New Haven, 1977). Frederick Merk, *Manifest Destiny and Mission in American History* (New York, 1963) is a classic study of expansionist ideology.

For Sabbatarianism, see Bertram Wyatt-Brown, "Prelude to Abolitionism: Sabbatarian Politics and the Rise of the Second Party System," *Journal of American History* 58 (1971): 316–341; James Rohrer, "Sunday Mails and the Church-State Theme in Jacksonian America," *Journal of the Early Republic* 7 (1987): 53–74; and Richard John, "Taking Sabbatarianism Seriously: The Postal System, the Sabbath, and the

Transformation of American Political Culture," *Journal of the Early Republic* 10 (1990): 517–567.

Two works on the temperance movement are essential: W. J. Rorabaugh, *The Alcoholic Republic: An American Tradition* (New York, 1979), and Ian Tyrrell, *Sobering Up: From Temperance to Prohibition in Antebellum America, 1800–1860* (Westport, Conn., 1979). For the roles of women and blacks in the antiliquor crusade, see Ian Tyrrell, "Women and Temperance in Antebellum America, 1830–1860," *Civil War History* 28 (1982): 128–152, and Donald Yacovone, "The Transformation of the Black Temperance Movement, 1827–1854: An Interpretation," *Journal of the Early Republic* 8 (1988): 281–297.

The best short treatment of abolitionism is James Brewer Stewart, *Holy Warriors: The Abolitionists and American Slavery* (New York, 1976). Also see Ronald Walters, *The Antislavery Appeal: American Abolitionism After 1830* (Baltimore, 1978). For black abolition, turn to Benjamin Quarles, *Black Abolitionists* (New York, 1969); Jane Pease and William Pease, *They Who Would Be Free: Blacks' Search for Freedom, 1830–1861* (Urbana, Ill., 1974); Carol George, *Segregated Sabbaths: Richard Allen and the Emergence of Independent Black Churches, 1760–1840* (New York, 1973); and Sernett, *Black Religion*. John McKivigan, *The War Against Proslavery Religion: Abolitionism and the Northern Churches, 1830–1865* (Ithaca, 1984) is essential for understanding the relationship between evangelicalism and abolition. For Northern denominations, see Donald Jones, *The Sectional Crisis and Northern Methodism: A Study in Piety, Political Ethics, and Civil Religion* (Metuchen, N.J., 1979); Richard Watkins, "The Baptists of the North and Slavery, 1856–1860," *Foundations* 13 (1970): 317–333; and Hugh Davis, "The New York *Evangelist*, New School Presbyterians and Slavery, 1837–1857," *American Pres-*

byterians 68 (1990): 14–23. The best study of antiabolitionist mobs is Leonard Richards, *"Gentlemen of Property and Standing": Anti-Abolition Mobs in Jacksonian America* (New York, 1970). For the proslavery argument, see Eugene Genovese and Elizabeth Fox-Genovese, "The Religious Ideals of Southern Slave Society," *Georgia Historical Quarterly* 70 (1986): 1–16, and Mitchell Snay, "American Thought and Southern Distinctiveness: The Southern Clergy and the Sanctification of Slavery," *Civil War History* 35 (1989): 311–328.

My thinking on Whig-Democrat ideological differences was influenced by Lawrence Frederick Kohl, *The Politics of Individualism: Parties and the American Character in the Jacksonian Era* (New York, 1989). For an excellent summary of the ethnocultural literature, read Robert Swierenga, "Ethnoreligious Political Behavior in the Mid-Nineteenth Century: Voting, Values, Cultures," in Mark Noll, ed., *Religion and American Politics: From the Colonial Period to the 1980s* (New York, 1990). For Methodists, see Richard Carwardine, "Methodist Ministers and the Second Party System," in Russell Richey and Kenneth Rowe, eds., *Rethinking Methodist History: A Bicentennial Historical Consultation* (Nashville, Tenn., 1985).

5. THE COMING OF THE LORD

For a quick overview of American millennialism, see James Patterson, "Changing Images of the Beast: Apocalyptic Conspiracy Theories in American History," *Journal of the Evangelical Theological Society* 31 (1988): 443–452. Dietrich G. Buss, "Meeting of Heaven and Earth: A Survey and Analysis of the Literature on Millennialism in America, 1965–1985," *Fides et Historia* 20 (1988): 5–28, provides a quick entry into the historiography of millennialism. For a general survey of nineteenth-century American thinking regarding the Second Coming, see Robert Whalen, "Millenarianism and Millennialism in America, 1790–1880" (Ph.D. dissertation, SUNY Stony Brook, 1971).

C. C. Goen, "Jonathan Edwards: A New Departure in Eschatology," *Church History* 28 (1959): 25–40, argues that Edwards was America's first major postmillennial thinker. Ernest Tuveson, *Redeemer Nation: The Idea of America's Millennial Role* (Chicago, 1968) traces millennial thought from early Christian history to the American Civil War. Two essential works on eighteenth-century American thought are Hatch, *Sacred Cause*, and Ruth Bloch, *Visionary Republic: Millennial Themes in American Thought, 1756–1800* (Cambridge, Mass., 1985). Jack Maddex, "Proslavery Millennialism: Social Eschatology in Antebellum Southern Calvinism," *American Quarterly* 31 (1979): 46–62, is an excellent discussion of Southern white postmillennialism. For the Union Prayer Meeting Revival, see Leonard Sweet, "'A Nation Born Again': The Union Prayer Meeting Revival and Cultural Revitalization," in Joseph Ban and Paul Dekar, eds., *In the Great Tradition, In Honor of Winthrop S. Hudson, Essays on Pluralism, Voluntarism, and Revivalism* (Valley Forge, Pa., 1982).

The comparative histories of British and American millenarianism is the subject of Ernest Sandeen, *The Roots of Fundamentalism: British and American Millenarianism, 1800–1930* (Chicago, 1970), and J. F. C. Harrison, *The Second Coming: Popular Millenarianism, 1780–1850* (New Brunswick, N.J., 1979). Although he does not use the term "folk apocalyptic," Michael Barkun discusses the social sources of apocalyptic thinking and compares Millerism and communitarianism in *Crucible of the Millennium: The Burned-Over*

District of New York in the 1840s (Syracuse, 1986). David Rowe, *Thunder and Trumpets: Millerites and Dissenting Religion in Upstate New York, 1800–1850* (Chico, Calif., 1985), and Ruth Doan, *The Miller Heresy, Millennialism, and American Culture* (Philadelphia, 1987) are essential studies of the Miller controversy. For a series of intriguing essays on Millerism, see Ronald Numbers and Jonathan Butler, eds., *The Disappointed: Millerism and Millenarianism in the Nineteenth Century* (Bloomington, Ind., 1987). For the career of a Southern premillennialist, see John Boles, "John Hersey: Dissenting Theologian of Abolitionism, Perfectionism, and Millennialism," *Methodist History* 14 (1976): 215–234. The connections between revivalism and premillennialism are explored in Jerald Brauer, "Revivalism and Millenarianism in America," in Ban and Dekar, *Great Tradition*.

For a brief description of antebellum black premillennialism, see Mathews, *Religion in the Old South*. Gayraud Wilmore, *Black Religion and Black Radicalism* (Garden City, N.Y., 1972) puts Prosser, Vesey, and Turner in the context of African American Christianity. Gerald Mullin, *Flight and Rebellion: Slave Resistance in Eighteenth-Century Virginia* (New York, 1972), and James Sidbury, "Gabriel's World: Race Relations in Richmond, Virginia, 1750–1810" (Ph.D. dissertation, Johns Hopkins University, 1991) examine the history and context of Gabriel's Insurrection. For Nat Turner, see Stephen Oates, *The Fires of Jubilee: Nat Turner's Fierce Rebellion* (New York, 1975).

For discussions of Civil War millennialism, turn to Tuveson, *Redeemer Nation*; James Moorhead, *American Apocalypse: Yankee Protestants and the Civil War, 1860–1869* (New Haven, 1978); and Walter Wiest, "Lincoln's Political Ethic: An Alternative to American Millennialism," *American Jour-*

nal of Theology and Philosophy 4 (1983): 116–126. W. J. Cash's classic *The Mind of the South* (New York, 1941), and John Lee Eighmy, *Churches in Cultural Captivity: A History of the Social Attitudes of Southern Baptists* (Knoxville, Tenn., 1972) briefly describe Southern Civil War rhetoric.

Index

A NOTE ON THE AUTHOR

Curtis D. Johnson was born in Duluth, Minnesota, studied at Moorhead State University, and received M.A. and Ph.D. degrees from the University of Minnesota. He is now associate professor of history at Mount Saint Mary's College in Emmitsburg, Maryland. Mr. Johnson has also written *Islands of Holiness: Rural Religion in Upstate New York, 1790–1860.*